UNEMPLOYMENT

Reprinted from
The Political Quarterly

UNEMPLOYMENT

edited by

BERNARD CRICK

METHUEN
London and New York

First published in 1981 by
Methuen & Co. Ltd
11 New Fetter Lane, London EC4P 4EE
Published in the USA by
Methuen & Co.
in association with Methuen, Inc.
733 Third Avenue, New York, NY 10017
© 1981 The Political Quarterly Publishing Co. Ltd
Printed in Great Britain by
Richard Clay (The Chaucer Press), Ltd
Bungay, Suffolk

ISBN 0416 32470 3

British Library Cataloguing in Publication Data

Crick, Bernard
  Unemployment.
  1. Unemployment—Great Britain
  I. Title
  331.13′7941   HD5767

  ISBN 0–416–32470–3 University paperback 758

CONTENTS

PREFACE

This book is a reprint of the January 1981 special number of *The Political Quarterly* together with Keith Middlemas's "Unemployment: the Past and Future of a Political Problem" from the previous issue. In fairness to the authors I must say that these articles are, for speed and economy, now printed unrevised, the publishers and ourselves believing in the urgency of giving this material wider circulation. Much has been written on unemployment and on the cruel folly of the Government's policies, but this symposium is unique in that most of the authors were asked to examine the regional differences. The conclusion is inescapable: that not merely is the industrial base of the country being destroyed but that the outlying regions suffer disproportionately. So much opinion in and of Britain is dominated by Whitehall, Westminster and Fleet Street; but the South-East (with some grim exceptions) suffers less than the rest of Britain and still neither perceives nor feels the depth of the crisis in the real industrial Britain of the regions. If we had updated these articles, the figures would only have been worse: overall in April 1981 there was 10·1 per cent unemployment as against 7·4 in September 1980; and the regional figures were:

S. East	7·1	E. Midlands	9·2	North	13·1
E. Anglia	8·2	Yorks &		Wales	13·0
S. West	9·1	Humber	10·6	Scotland	12·0
W. Midlands	12·0	N. West	12·1	N. Ireland	16·4

The tendencies and the relationships have not changed, nor have the structural and cultural factors.

I sadly chose this sombre theme to mark my retirement after fifteen years in *The Political Quarterly*'s editorial chair, handing on to David Watt and Rudolf Klein. So I carry responsibility for all omissions, most of all a regret that I did not commission a piece—thinking with hindsight of the Brixton disturbances —specifically on black unemployment. But I am wholly unapologetic at reopening the debate about whether Britain at its best can remain a centralised state based on London and the elite mentality of the London, Oxford, Cambridge triangle.

BERNARD CRICK

COMMENTARY

PERSPECTIVES ON UNEMPLOYMENT

WE asked most of the contributors to this special number to write on the extent of unemployment in a region of the United Kingdom, on its social effect, and on its probable political consequences. We also asked for certain special topics to be covered, notably youth unemployment and trade union wage bargaining. Most of the articles are deliberately descriptive and informative. While some in fact contain arguments about what should be done, only two contributors were asked to address themselves principally to what should and could be done, Professor Maurice Peston on the economics and Austin Mitchell, M.P. on the politics of unemployment. Readers will notice one obvious omission from the regions included, the South East. This omission is deliberate.

Consider these figures. In September 1980 there were, according to the Department of Employment, the following percentages of unemployment in the regions—with a national average of 7·4 per cent.

S. East	4·9	E. Midlands	6·6	North	10·2
E. Anglia	5·8	Yorks &		Wales	10·3
S. West	6·8	Humber	7·6	Scotland	9·7
W. Midlands	8·0	N. West	9·2	N. Ireland	13·3

What is glaringly obvious is that the further one goes from London the worse the situation becomes. And within some of the worst-hit regions there are area variations, such as Liverpool, Glasgow, Tyneside and Belfast which reach well over double the national average. This may not surprise people, for such regional variations are part of our economic history. But they are also part of our political and cultural history. The outlying regions are those with the least political effect generally, those most easy to ignore in electoral terms—especially when Conservative governments are in power. And the "peripheral regions", to give a geographical expression a realistic and terrible moral connotation, are also those which culturally are the least understood and perceived by the administrative, political and opinion-forming elite of the South East, meaning mainly those who work in London.

It has long been thought, not merely morally but also politically and prudentially, that the modern State needs to ensure the welfare of its inhabitants, not merely to provide for their safety and defence

1

and their formal equality before the law. Why is the danger of such vast unemployment not seen, as well as its immorality and social destructiveness? The answer must lie in the fact that in the capital city 4.9 per cent. unemployment is hardly perceptible, unless one happens to live in, say, North Kensington or Brixton or Hackney, which most of the opinion-makers and administrators (to put it mildly) do not. When it is so difficult to get a plumber, a char-woman or a window-cleaner in spite of " so much unemployment ", the whole thing, they feel and perceive, must be an illusion. And two decades at least of soft living and easyriding have made those in jobs, especially in the top jobs (like many of our readers), simply not want to know, they wish to disbelieve it, those two million moving towards three million unemployed. The Chairman of the C.B.I. had to make a winter journey (but to his honour he did) before he became convinced that in the experience of the regions there is a pressing danger (quite beyond adjustments of the interest rate and the " strength " of sterling, etc.) of sheer ungovernability. This may not take the form of demonstrations, riots, civil dis-obedience (and beyond?). Several of our contributors candidly refuse to scare us in this all-too-human way. It may take the form of these millions of people simply dropping out of the polity, simply ceasing to be citizens: on the one hand, ignored by a tough-minded Government, even by self-protective trade unions; on the other, a population removed from the possibility of influence, con-trol, usefulness. Professor Ridley's surmise is all too likely to prove true: that permanently unemployed young people (white and black) will not fall prey to " political extremists ", but rather enter into violent, random, delinquent protest, a *Clockwork Orange* world rather than one of political stirrings. Would that they did fall prey to the Revolutionary Socialists or the National Front, that might stir some normal pre-emptive political reactions. What is more likely to happen is that their " mindless " delinquency (quite rational in their hopeless circumstances) will simply evoke more cries from the employed of the need for " law and order ", for more to be spent on the police force and less on the social services: a vicious circle of irrelevant class aggression. Such will be the social consequence of what the Labour Party and C.B.I. and anti-Thatcher Tories are beginning to call the sacrifice of industry to capital, the all-out attack on inflation, even at the cost of productivity.

Because of the lack of political response to mass unemployment and the flagrant indifference of public opinion, our symposium begins quite simply with an account of what it feels like to be unem-

2

ployed. Some people are sceptical about Jeremy Seabrook's Orwell-like technique of being the participant observer; they prefer aggregate data instead. But aggregate data do not reveal the qualitative effect, indeed cannot show how people are likely to react. It does not matter precisely how typical some of the people he interviews are: the disturbing point is that they exist at all. And one of his comments on the contrast between the 1930s and today worries like a nightmare and shifts political perspectives:

"In the 1930s, those who wanted to work had a sense that they had only to wait before their labour would be required again. . . . Unemployment impaired their sense of worth, assailed their dignity, denied them and those they loved adequate food and comfort. But it didn't rob them of the skills themselves. Now . . . there is a terminal sense of the extinction of work itself. Something elusive and despairing pervades those towns and cities which were built only for the sake of their purpose in the old industrial processes. It is as though the working class were being wounded in its very reason for existence, work itself."

Fred Ridley's contribution is of profound importance. It is fair to say that he did not begin his work for unemployed young people on Merseyside with the perspectives he now holds. The best way of avoiding these perspectives, perhaps, is not to look and not to know, deliberate suppression; otherwise one observes, he says: " passive alienation . . . a generation idle and frustrated because unemployed; rejected by employers, thus alienated; concentrated in certain districts where the environment itself is grim—not revolution, but simply undirected violence and pointless destruction ". 85 per cent. of unemployed young people on Merseyside, he reminds us, recently replied to a survey that they had no interest in politics. And Ben Pimlott points out that in the North East there are more than four times as many unemployed for each notified job vacancy as in the South East. It could be that politicians will now arise capable of stirring the unemployed and " the regions " against the political and cultural dominance of the South East; and they could be, would have to be, as tough towards private property rights as the present Government has been towards the need (the right?) to work in their crazy, single-minded, monetarist obsession with inflation—at whatever cost, it seems, to employment or industrial production.

John Osmond, writing on South Wales, where of all places disorder might well be expected, reaches similar conclusions to Fred Ridley. He weighs the present evidence and finds that even as South Wales becomes deindustrialised, rioting and extremist politics are unlikely. He is a responsible political journalist. It says much about the situation in the regions that such matters have to be weighed.

And, after all, it is through deliberate Government policy (Austin Mitchell scarcely exaggerates) that unemployment has come to that pitch. I find that I myself, supposed by many to be a Paladin of moderates, am beginning to consider the thesis of the philosopher Ted Honderich's recent book *Violence for Equality*. He easily dismisses most arguments for violence, but in so far as most large inequalities are deliberately maintained by government, there remains, he considers, always a residual possibility of justifying violence when such imposed inequalities correlate to different life expectancies among the social classes. The argument is difficult and esoteric, as well as disturbing; but Honderich points out that governments have a greater opportunity (and moral duty) to end misery without violence than most revolutionaries to create justice through violence. Government must come to its senses.

Government policy has brought us to the point where such thoughts cannot be suppressed, unless we never look further afield than the placid and affluent Home Counties. And when high unemployment and nationalism coincide, it is gross political folly to think that the " United Kingdom " or devolution question has been settled; contributors from the other nations make that abundantly clear. It is perhaps mildly obsessive of Stephen Maxwell to have treated unemployment in Scotland almost solely in terms of its effect on the fortunes of his own Scottish National Party. Not all Scots will welcome this. (An icily clear statement of Scotland's economic condition is to be found in the October 1980 number of the Fraser of Allander Institute's *Quarterly Economic Commentary*, University of Strathclyde.) But basically Maxwell is right. Scotland is one of the worst hit regions of the British Isles, and special attention is only given to her needs and traditions when she acts, or threatens to act, in—from a United Kingdom point of view—an aberrant political manner.

More gently, Professor Norman Gibson, writing on Northern Ireland, quotes Keynes to show: (a) that state intervention for full employment is possible, and (b) to remind us that this may not be compatible with the highest wage rates possible:

" If we decide that the interests of justice and charity require that the income of the working class should be higher than that which they receive from the economic machine, then we must, so to speak, subscribe to that end. Taxation is a measure of compulsory subscription, and the subscription must be spread over the whole community. But if that subscription is to fall solely on a particular body of employers then we must not be surprised if the level of employment and output is below what it should be."

4

Part of the blame the late Labour Government must take is not just for their partial acceptance of monetarism but their political cowardice in not fighting Mrs. Thatcher hard enough when she promised tax cuts. If we want full employment and a Welfare State, a high, graduated income tax on those in profitable employment is inevitable and justifiable; and if nobody likes paying it even on the margin, that is a different proposition from saying that people will not pay it if they think the cause is just, or even that they would be too frightened of the consequences if they did not. Mr. Callaghan failed his party on that—little or nothing to do with the " Left ", " Right ", " Democratic " or " Centrist " disputes within the Party. And the Labour Party retreated from an incomes policy rather than try to produce a socialist incomes policy—or quite simply to control the top as well as the bottom (what I long argued for in these columns: a " Mini-Max " incomes policy).

Yet things have gone so far that Maurice Peston can argue here that: " it is a measure of the mess that we are in that with the best will in the world it is hard to believe that unemployment could get down to a million by 1990 ". Simply consider, he argues, the number of jobs that would have to be created in each year to get back to old expectations, especially when there is not merely laying off (recession) but now large-scale closing down (depression). (Stan Taylor's article on the deindustrialisation of the West Midlands is grimly impressive on this point.) The political and economic situation is obviously one in which welfare will have to be created from social security for many years rather than from any real hopes of job creation on the scale needed. The Gross National Product will depend more on capital-intensive industry, even if we can get the bankers off our shoulders. And this will mean higher levels of income tax. And the unpopularity of this among new taxpayers—as the last election showed. And the positively weird state of British public opinion about unemployment and poverty.

Four years ago, a comparative study was conducted on *The Perception of Poverty in Europe* (published by the Commission in 1977). Most people in Europe had a fairly dour and common-sense attitude to poverty, that it was caused by involuntary unemployment and by initial poor home conditions. But one category of respondents was labelled " cynics ". These were people who rarely if ever see poverty: " If poor people exist, it is because they are lazy or lack will power . . . there is no great need to reduce social inequality and the public authorities are doing enough—if not too much ". Over all the EEC countries, 14 per cent. of respondents were " cynics ", but in Britain

5

a massive 27 per cent.—10 per cent. higher than the next country, Germany. And recent surveys tell us that *most* people in jobs believe that there are jobs to be had if the unemployed bestir themselves! As with their stories of welfare-state scroungers, the popular Press have a lot to answer for. Where else could these stupid and distinctively British stereotypes have come from? If there are to be alternative economic policies, political leaders have to establish, boldly and patiently, that unemployment is involuntary, and that we face disaster, either economic or political or both, if people cannot be got back to work. If that is not possible, their life chances must be rendered much the same as for those in work—which means high taxation towards redistribution of incomes.

Keith Middlemas, the Conservative historian, wrote a remarkable article in the last number of THE POLITICAL QUARTERLY, which was really the prelude to this Special Number. It concluded:

". . . what will Britain look like after even three years of two million unemployed? Divisions which for half a century governments have tried to abolish will show nakedly, between the two geographical Englands, with Scotland, Wales and Northern Ireland on the periphery, like the Italian Mezzogiorno; between those in work and the unemployed; between the mature and the young, between white and black. They already exist. If they are heightened by the sort of political conflict allied to a capital/labour antithesis which nearly every Conservative leader since Baldwin has tried to prevent, or by an unthinking and indiscriminate assault on trade unionism which confuses structural backwardness with moral turpitude, or by an intolerant repudiation of the post-war consensus rather than a reasoned attempt to find out what went wrong, then it will recall the old tag: '*Ubi solitudinem faciunt, pacem appellant*'—where they make a desert, they call it peace."

Perhaps it will be more easy to carry out alternative economic policies, if attempted by the reviving Labour Party, than actually to recognise their need.

BERNARD CRICK.

UNEMPLOYMENT NOW AND IN THE 1930s

JEREMY SEABROOK

In an old-fashioned parlour in a house in Sunderland, an old man reaches down a painted biscuit tin, in which he keeps, not family photographs, but pictures of the people of Sunderland taken during the depression of the 1930s. " I take these pictures out sometimes to remind other people. I don't need reminding myself. There's not a day goes by but what I feel the bitterness and shame at what this country did to millions of its working people." The photographs, faded and cracked with age, fan out across a threadbare chenille tablecloth. He indicates a young woman with braided hair and a graceful plinth of neck: " She came from a TB family. You knew who the TB families were, you knew you had not to marry into them if you wanted your children to survive. She died when she was nineteen." There is a picture of a misty street, with a cluster of men on the corner, hands in pockets, bodies arched against the cold. A man looks unsmilingly at the camera, flat cap, muffler parted to reveal collarless shirt. " He was a miner. After the general strike he never found work again. He cut his throat one afternoon in 1931. It was July. I can remember it like yesterday. I came home from school and found him. He'd left a message on the looking glass written with a cake of soap, saying he was sorry. He was my father. . . ."

A council flat in the same town, October 1980. A young man with a beard, a few threads of silver in his dark hair, tries to pacify his nine-month-old son, while his wife, 19 and pregnant with their third child, pushes her three-year-old out of the door onto the landing, and tells her not to come back until she is ready to say she is sorry. The child starts to scream, and the mother buries her face in her hands. The room is piled with washing, clothes, towels and nappies, a few scraps of children's toys. The double bed and cot leave room for nothing but a sideboard. The young couple live with the girl's parents in their two-bedroomed flat. The electricity has been cut off in their own house, and the arrears of rent have reached several hundred pounds. The husband went to London to find work.

* The author has written *The Underprivileged* (Longmans, 1967), *City Close-Up* (A. Lane, 1971), and *What Went Wrong?* (Gollancz, 1978).

He was offered only low-paid catering jobs, but could find nowhere for his family to live. He came back yet more heavily in debt and with an even more overwhelming feeling of failure. " My wife has known nothing but debt and poverty ever since we've been married . . . I ought to feel glad, being able to spend so much time with my kids while they're young. But I just feel shame that I can't provide them with any of the things they need. We have no life together. I've even stopped looking for work. Some days I feel like topping myself, I'm not kidding. . . . If there's no hope for me, what chance will there be for them? Life won't be worth living, I feel like taking them with me. . . ."

" I pity those who haven't got work now. When we were unemployed, people were generally more sympathetic to us than they are now. When we marched, there were always a few who stood on the pavement calling us Commies and Reds, but on the whole, people's goodwill was with you. Nobody ever called us scroungers; I'd never heard the word layabout. But now, they make you feel it's your own fault. But what appals me now is that they don't have hope, and we did. We felt, not only that work would pick up again, but that time was on our side. We still saw a future possibility for socialism. We knew the Labour Party hadn't reached the height of its development, in spite of the setbacks of the two Labour governments. We were still waiting. But not now. The young have no such hope now. Their only hopes are centred on individual salvation— the dream of the pools, the big Bingo win. We hoped for the whole of the working class, not just for ourselves. . . . (Man, 70.)

" Well you come out of school, you might do a bit of thieving, you know you have to have money, and you'll more or less turn to anything to get it. I wouldn't knife people, I haven't got the bottle to do that. But round here the rule is if it moves, pick it up and sell it. Loads of kids will nick things, anything made of metal, bits of cars, copper or lead off roofs, and sell it for scrap. Even good things, you might get a fridge worth a hundred quid, but you sell it just for scrap value, because that's the only way you can get rid of it with no questions asked. That and lining—just cut two ends of a washing line. Only trouble is, so many people have done it, the price of rags has dropped to nothing. . . . The future? I don't think about it. Get pissed, sniff a bit of glue, have a fight. . . . What else is there? " (Boy, 17.)

" What kind of a Christmas am I going to give my kids? It makes you feel terrible. I'm ashamed to face them. . . . What kind

of a childhood are they getting? They'll look back and curse me."
(Man, 30.)

" I wish people had a bit more of the spirit they had then, in the
1930s. Where I lived, there was a lot of poverty. But my mother was
a good neighbour. The neighbours used to visit and comfort each
other. And you know, the feckless were more or less carried by
those who were a bit more careful. Nobody would ever let bairns
suffer. The poor weren't all dumped on just one or two estates like
they are now, where people can point them out and call them
rubbish and scroungers. The poorest weren't segregated, they lived
cheek by jowl with canny folk. There was a wider humanity
then. . . ." (Man, 70s.)

" I feel very disappointed. When I was young, I felt Christianity
offered something; it could change people's lives. But as I grew up,
I saw it didn't make any difference. People stayed poor, unemployment got worse; and those who were in the Church seemed just as
bigoted and unjust as our enemies. So I joined the Labour Party.
That became my life. I thought: ' That's the way to do it, you've
got to get organised, get our people into Parliament, then it'll all
change '. I gave everything to the Party. Young people saw a glim-
mer of light then, they had something to work for. Now they hope
they might get rich; but that isn't an alternative, now is it? " (Man,
60s.)

" As a child, I was always cold. Cold and hungry. The money
there went on rent, coal and food, in that order. My mother died
when I was seven, and my oldest sister brought us up. But the fire
was always kept going. When we went to bed, we might have the
shelf out of the oven wrapped in flannel, or the hand-iron, wrapped
in some old material. It wasn't very comfortable to sleep with, but it
was warm. And then we had each other to cuddle up to. . . . We
thought it was a treat when my sister could afford a ninepenny
wrap-up from the butcher at the week-end—a bit of neck-end, a
sausage and some black pudding. It was like Christmas Day then.
. . ." (Woman, 70s.)

" Well, you must remember, the thirties were a very defeated time
on the domestic front. That was why so many people would think
no wrong of the Soviet Union. But there was despair in those years.
In this town, I've seen men disintegrate, weep with shame because
they couldn't provide for their wives and families. To me, things
are not so different now as we go into the eighties. It's not that we
had the defeat of the general strike; our equivalent is the winter of
discontent, as they called it. That was very much a public spectacle,

wasn't it, a way of discrediting the Labour movement, by showing that workers were heartless and callous. It leaves a taste of defeat somehow. . . . The feeling reminds me a bit of those years after 1926, although thank God people aren't so poor. But you know, that seemed like a final defeat to us then. It left bitterness. But of course nothing is ever final. It's a bit like the end of the book *The Grapes of Wrath*, do you remember, where the mother says: ' We are the people. We go on for ever.' " (Man, 80.)

" If you've got no work, everything seems to mock you. It might be me, but you feel it. The television, the adverts, everything. The papers are full of the lives of millionaires, the shops are full of things you can't afford. . . . It makes you feel humiliated . . . it destroys your self-respect. . . . Your kids can't have what others do, it makes you feel you're a failure. . . . You start to listen to the tone of the telly commercials, and you realise they're not just inviting you to buy, they're orders—It's get this, have that, buy the other. You start to hate yourself because you feel out of step, shabby, unworthy. You can't afford to go out on a Saturday night, so you stay in; me and the wife, we play cards for pennies, share one bottle of Brown; then you turn the television on, and there's Parkinson, chatting up all the rich and the successful and the self-satisfied. You can't get away from it. It follows you everywhere, makes you feel worse than a criminal. . . ." (Man, 40s.)

A DHSS Appeal tribunal. A man of about 50, dressed in a brown jacket shiny with age, a frayed crew-neck sweater, thin trousers. His hair is sparse, his eyes anxious and mobile. He sits in the basement of the Rechabite Hall, in the waiting-room. His appointment is for 10 o'clock; but so is that of others in the waiting-room. At 12.15, he is still waiting. " I worked for 25 years in the pit, and I never had a day off work; but then I got arthritis of the spine. I'm diabetic and I have bronchitis. I have to wear a steel corset for the spine. I get £40 in invalidity benefit, and of that I give £14 to my wife and the children; we're separated. I have a little house, and the mortgage outstanding on it is only about £100. It's badly in need of repair, it's falling down, but I can't do anything about it except watch it deteriorate. I can't eat starchy food because of the diabetes. I'm supposed to eat meat and fruit, but how can I on £26 a week? I can't buy clothes, when things wear out I can't replace them. I feel shabby. My only outings are to the hospital. All I do is walk my dog round the block. I can't go to the club to buy a drink for anyone; I can't even afford one for myself. I've come to ask for some extra money for basic repairs to the house. If they refuse me again, I'll have to sell it and go into a council-house. I get very depressed and lonely. I've no hope ever of working again. So when I look into the future all I see is myself getting older, shabbier and poorer. I'd be better off if I was in gaol. I've never done anything wrong, but I feel ashamed and guilty all the time. It makes you feel useless, you feel you've no right to exist. Some days it makes you angry, but then others, you feel sorry for yourself, you sit at home and cry, but nobody sees you. I don't know if I'll get any extra money today. It depends on how they feel. If they're in a good mood I might; if not, I'll just have to sell my house and then hand over the money in rent until I'm just about a pauper again. It was to get out of poverty that I struggled and worked like I did; not to get shoved back there again. . . ."

" People say to me: ' Oh your life is one long holiday. . . '. I've not had a job for two years, and with a police record, I'm not likely to get one very easily. I stay in bed most days till about one o'clock; there's nothing to get up for. You'd be surprised how much you can sleep if you try. When I wake up and think of all the hours I've got to fill I think ' Oh Christ '. You find yourself looking forward to when the kids' programmes come on telly. That's when you realise just how far you've started to rot. The estate where I live is a bit posher than some of them, a lot of the people are going to buy their houses. You feel conspicuous. If they see you hanging round in the daytime, they look at you as if you were something the cat sicked up on their new carpet. . . ." (Man, 30s.)

" They talk on television about the leisure society. God help us, that's all I can say. If there's one thing the lads round here don't need it's leisure. Leisure means institutionalised unemployment. For ever. What a nightmare ' In loving memory of the working class. Fell asleep around 1980. . . ' " (Community worker, 20s.)

The Easy Response

The easy response is that it is less painful to be out of work in the 1980s than it was in the 1930s, because of the protection afforded by the state against destitution. But the comparison with the 1930s is misleading in almost every way. The suggestion of the 1930s, for all the horrible memories it evokes, does offer at the same time a vaguely comforting view: however unpleasant it is, it is at least familiar. We have been through it all before. It shows there is nothing new under the sun. It isn't hard to find people on the Left who feel vindicated by what they see happening now, those whose warnings over the years that capitalism hasn't changed have found no response. It seems to prove to them that the last 30 years have been simply an aberration, just as they have been saying. But despite many superficial similarities, it is not a return to the 1930s that the capitalist process requires now. The comparisons are trite and obvious; and they conceal the epic nature of the changes occurring in the working class in this last quarter of the century.

So does the context in which mass unemployment is recurring for the first time in 40 years. The considerable sums which many workers have received in redundancy payments, combined with all the optimistic talk coming from the media about the promise of microtechnology, seem to offer a prospect of endless leisure and freedom from toil. A popular confusion seems to have arisen between leisure and redundancy; the hedonistic values associated with the consumer economy mask the fact that large sections of the working class are being relieved of any sense of function or purpose. A steel worker, who spent his £11,000 redundancy money in less than a year, said: " We had a smashing time. We went all over America. We went to visit our cousins who went to Canada during the depression. We were the ones with the money to flash around, they thought we were rich. I said to them: ' I bet you wish you'd stayed at home now '. I didn't tell them. . . . And then, when we got back, we had a new kitchen fitted, we bought a three-piece. . . . We said: ' Let tomorrow look after itself, we shall probably all be blown to kingdom come anyway '. This, together with the opportunities for fiddling, the unofficial jobs and private transactions, helps to blunt the effect of disemployment, obscure the pain of rejection. Some of the ways in which those out of work contrive to help themselves are ingenious. Most are probably trifling and don't amount to very much; but I heard of one man who drove a big lorry across Europe, and who sold it and its cargo in Italy and then got his mate to beat him about a bit, so he could claim it had been hijacked.

For most people, however, any moment of euphoria is brief, and covers only the instant of job loss. As time goes by, the unemployed, however numerous they are, begin to feel isolated. When savings and redundancy money run out, they discover the growing poverty is not assuaged by any pooling of resources, by the sharing of hardship which occurred in the 1930s. They begin to feel the loss of the old supportive networks in the working-class streets. More than this; since the poor law ceased to exist 32 years ago, its values and attitudes have been enthusiastically absorbed by many of those who had previously suffered its cruel disciplines, and the unemployed find themselves the objects of a public opinion that sees them as scroun-

gers, idlers and shirkers. " There's work for them as want it ";
" Why should anybody work when they can get more on the dole ".
In the East End of London, of all places, I heard one woman say
solemnly that they should bring back the workhouse.

The sense of loneliness which many of those without work men-
tion is reinforced by the imperatives of buying and selling to which
they continue to be subjected. Images of wealth and abundance pour
from the media and the newspapers, making no concession to
failure and imperfection. Capitalism continues to be projected as
provider of abundance and fulfilment; and this is vastly at odds
with the way it was perceived in the depressed working-class areas
in the 1930s. It is perhaps this change, more than any other, which
makes people turn against each other rather than identify the source
of their suffering in anything connected with the images of plenty
that still flow from the great shopping centres which dominate every
town and city. In fact, the endless promise implicit in the capitalist
capacity for production of all that is good and desirable has been
a major contributory factor to the quiescence of working people in
the face of the present upheavals. For one thing, it has extinguished
the vision of any alternative. The possibility of even imagining any
radical change has been effectively blocked for most of the working
class—even of the unemployed themselves; and this was certainly
not true of the 1930s. " Then, we might have been corroded by
hunger and idleness, but we were moved by the excitement of
working for the Labour Party. We were committed, heart and soul.
The hope for change had not been dashed. . . ." (Man, 60s.)

In the 1930s, hope remained public and collective; whereas in the
1980s there is room only for individual fantasy—the big pools win,
a lucky night at Bingo, the sudden access to money of individuals.
Capitalism now owns even the visions of a better life, and it parades
them tirelessly; and perhaps this is why observers are puzzled by the
passivity, the acceptance, even the indifference of the majority of
those out of work towards their own situation. It is often said grimly
by trades unionists and Labour politicians that people won't put up
with the indignity of being out of work as they did in the 1930s; but
in fact they do. The anger and frustration tend to turn inwards.
People turn on each other, or even on themselves. Violence, family
breakdown, mental illness are part of the price people pay. That
the causes for some of these things are not sought in any political
context but are kept firmly in the realm of the personal, is a measure
of the cleansing of the system that has occurred. I spoke to a man
who, after three years on the dole in Glasgow, ran away to New-

...e on Tyne, just to get away from his family. " I couldn't stand ... pressure. I hated being at home. I felt useless. I was no good to them. They're better off without me. I've four kids, the eldest is nine now. But when I was there, I was shouting at them all the time. I never spoke to them in a normal tone of voice. I could feel myself losing control. One night I got that mad, the baby wouldn't stop crying, I went to pick her up, but I knew if I did, that would be it. I'd 've broken her like a doll. That was it. I had to get out. It makes me feel bad, what I did. But I don't know what I would have done if I'd stayed there. It's best for all of us. . . ." (Man, 28.) Personal failure and not economic processes are seen by many as the cause of their suffering; and this feeds an already fragile sense of worth in the working-class people, whose experience is not validated anywhere in the media, and whose skills and functions are being eroded in a more dramatic way than has probably ever happened before.

This is, perhaps, the most profound and damaging influence upon working people in the last 30 years, of which the present surge in unemployment is only a more virulent manifestation.

In the 1930s, those who wanted work had a sense that they had only to wait before their labour would be required again. When they talk of those years, they evoke the idle machinery, the eerie silence over shipyard and pithead. Unemployment impaired their sense of worth, assailed their dignity, denied them and those they loved adequate food and comfort. But it didn't rob them of the skills themselves. Now, on the other hand, there is a terminal sense of the extinction of work itself. Something elusive and despairing pervades those towns and cities which were built only for the sake of their purpose in the old industrial processes. It is as though the working class were being wounded in its very reason for existence, work itself.

We are told that this is a continuing process, and always has been. The working class is simply evolving. As old skills decay, new ones are generated. We must adapt and change. This may be true. But it is at least equally possible that such an assertion may serve only to buttress another kind of complacency. If we believe that there is nothing new in the contemporary situation, we capitulate to those forces that are tending to erode the whole sense of identity and meaning of the working class. As we are told that new functions and new purposes will arise for the working class, we are informed at the same time that there has been a quantum leap in technological development which means that fewer and fewer people will be required in the future to do less and less work. In this context, the promise of limitless leisure, as a kind of reward to the working class for its secular toil, is not very reassuring. When trade union leaders and Tory Ministers unite to announce the end of the Puritan work ethic, and when we consider how the socialist alternative has been devalued, obscured, undermined by the promises of abundance in which the working class has been nurtured for 30 years, we should perhaps be on our guard. It all suggests a very different possibility: that capitalism has glimpsed the way to render its working class, if not exactly expendable, at least sufficiently functionless to become even more subordinate than it has always been. It certainly isn't the 1930s all over again. It is the prospect of a more abject servitude than that. What the disciplines of destitution and hunger could not achieve may be brought about far more effectively through a destroyed sense of purpose and function masquerading as increased leisure. The only imaginable working-class response to that would be the kind of violence we have seen in the United States, and to a lesser extent among the young here—" mindless " violence, racial conflict, the rioting and looting—an anger detached from any conscious political objective. This remains a real danger; and at the same time it is a measure of the growing political impotence of the working class.

Retired miner, 60: " When I see Ma Thatcher talking about her nuclear power stations, I know what she really means. She wants to replace dependency on coal with nuclear power because she wants to bust the power of the miners. Once she's done that, she's destroyed the heart of the working class. That's what she's all about, make no mistake about it. They want to break us. Then they'll have it all their own way, won't they? "

VIEW FROM A DISASTER AREA: UNEMPLOYED YOUTH IN MERSEYSIDE

F. F. RIDLEY

" WE looked out from the entrance of Lime Street Station and saw a city which seemed to be slowly dying, unloved and unsung, in the Depression of the nineteen-twenties." Thus Helen Forrester in her harrowing memories, *Twopence to Cross the Mersey*. Liverpool has been much sung since then, even if not more loved, but songs are not enough. Mrs. Forrester's bankrupt father came to Liverpool to seek work because " having lived for years in prosperous, southern market-towns, he could not visualise what the Depression was doing to the north of England ". What is happening in Liverpool now has not been grasped by our masters in the South either. Knowing the facts, of course, is not enough. The politicians and civil servants who come up for the day to attend meetings or even to " meet the people " return without any real understanding of life by the Mersey. For that one has to live here. It is one of the worst faults of our system of government that decision-makers inhabit Westminster and Whitehall. The Celtic fringe probably suffers less from the " internal colonialism " which some political scientists have recently discovered than does Merseyside.

" Liverpool is quite simply a disaster area for school-leavers ", stated the *Education Guardian* recently. Liverpool is not just worse off than other cities in the current depression: it was worse off before and it will be worse off after. Some, indeed, say it is a dying city. One is not supposed to say that. The local authority has instructed its staff to present a cheerful face for fear of frightening off such investors as may still be around. Warts-and-all accounts on TV and in the Press arouse anger for the same reason. It is nonsense, however, to think that massive private investment will come our way through glossy public relations. Better face the truth. What that is, of course, cannot be predicted with certainty. Economists—the wisest fools in Christendom—are never reliable. Local interests, for their part, have perhaps cried wolf too often, but the

* The author is Professor of Political Theory and Institutions, University of Liverpool. He was Chairman of the Job Creation Programme in Merseyside and is Vice-Chairman of the M.S.C.'s Special Programmes Board for the area.

16

wolf does seem to be blowing our house down. One Liverpool firm, in a recent Chamber of Commerce survey, wrote: " We have survived two world wars, the blitz and the depression of the 1930s; I wonder whether we will last out the next twelve months? " Liverpool's plight needs to be taken seriously, not noted as a matter of statistics but experienced. Not just for the sake of Merseysiders, youth above all, but because the whole country will have to pay the price of its long-term malaise otherwise.

Bermuda Triangle of British Capitalism

Should one start with statistics or impressions? Impressions are hard to convey unless one has the gifts of Mrs. Forrester. They may also be dismissed by the unsympathetic as unreliable. So let me start with figures about unemployment. Unemployment is rising so quickly now that such figures are bound to be well below the present rate, but that does not make them any less significant, because even dated figures show the special position of this area. In January 1980 the unemployment rate stood at 12·7 per cent.—higher than in any of the other six major conurbations and well above the 7·6 per cent. for the North West and the 5·9 per cent. for the country as a whole. Liverpool has (1) a higher level of permanent unemployment than elsewhere even in good times; (2) a higher level of cyclical unemployment, depression hitting it worse than elsewhere; and (3) a deteriorating position compared to the country as a whole, a steady loss of jobs widening the gap ever further.

A recent study described Merseyside as the Bermuda triangle of British capitalism. While the massive rise in unemployment in the last year has been the result of a national crisis, the longer term causes lie in the structure of the local economy. Liverpool grew as a port, but there has been a continuous decline in port-related activities: the end of the slave trade started the rot, followed by the disappearance of the transatlantic passenger trade and the cotton trade. The town's manufacturing base has always been relatively small. This means there has also been little in the way of skilled work, engineering for example, and thus no pool of skilled labour to attract new employers. The area is also vulnerable because the manufacturing sector is dominated to a greater extent than most other regions by a small number of national or international firms. Closures have been announced almost every month for years now, not just because of the current " shake-out " of labour but the result of rationalisation policies decided in London or abroad by faceless directors who have no personal connection with Merseyside.

17

The image of Merseyside—workers militant or bloody-minded—is often used to explain why the blow falls here rather than somewhere else. Statistics do not support this view (Department of Employment figures show that Merseyside comes sixth in the inter-city strike league, and that only because nationally strike-prone industries are over-represented here) but businessmen are not always rational. A more rational explanation is that Liverpool is being by-passed in the restructuring of British industry because of its geographical position. The current policy is to encourage the growth of small, locally-based firms instead, though it is hard to see this happening on a sufficient scale. Liverpool is also badly placed when it comes to developing the white-collar sectors of employment. Regional offices, for example, tend to gravitate to Manchester which is only 30 miles away. What has grown in Liverpool has been the public sector of employment: some 30 per cent. of those employed in the City work for central and local government, the health service and public enterprise—yet another factor making Liverpool particularly vulnerable in the present climate.

Workplaces are disappearing all the time and there seems little reason to expect market forces to halt the trend. It seems almost inevitable in an economy where decisions are made by directors pursuing (quite properly) the financial interests of their companies regardless of social consequences or, indeed, of the fact that their companies, too, ultimately pay the costs of depressed areas. PR by local government to attract new industries and central government measures to encourage them are marginal. It is hard to visualise a reversal of Liverpool's decline except in a planned economy. The unemployed could move elsewhere, of course—at least when the economy picks up again. But there has already been an outflow of young, able-bodied, skilled and semi-skilled workers and this simply exacerbates inner-city problems caused by an unbalanced population. And should young people, in any case, be encouraged to seek work elsewhere? Mrs. Thatcher recently said that people should not expect to find work where they *happened* to live. That not only shows her divorce from the realities of life (families that depend on more than one bread-winner cannot easily move); it shows her own lack of roots in conservatism: what of community links and family ties as the basis of a well-ordered society? Work will have to be brought to the workers despite fashionable economic arguments to the contrary.

Let me turn back to figures as a measure of the local disaster. A recent study by our Planning Office showed that the Department

18

of Employment statistics seriously underestimate total unemployment in the region. They show the number of persons registered as unemployed as a percentage of insured employees (including those registered unemployed). The base figure of insured employees is drawn from a census several years old, however, and the steady decline in permanent workplaces since then is ignored; ignored also is the fact that many are seeking work without being registered (*e.g.* married women not eligible for unemployment benefits) and that a large number of young people on temporary government schemes are also seeking proper jobs. In mid-1980, when the official figure for the Liverpool Travel To Work Area was around 13 per cent., something like 22 per cent. of those seeking work in Liverpool (not quite the same area) could not find a job. This was something like 17 per cent. of the total population—and unemployment figures as a percentage of the total population may give a better picture of the social consequences. (These figures should doubtless be reduced to take account of those engaged in the " grey economy "— but the opportunities for earning a living in this way in Liverpool are almost certainly less than in more prosperous parts of the country.)

The Planning Office also showed that the official statistics masked the dramatic incidence of unemployment for certain groups and localities. In one inner-city planning district unemployment ran at 37 per cent., in another at 31 per cent.; on one very large housing estate it reached 40 per cent. (and all this does not take account of unregistered job-seekers). Figures are no better in certain outer-city council estates. There employment often depends on a few large factories, and closures have an even more dramatic effect on the community. In Speke, for example, some 45 per cent. of the adult population depend on the state in one way or another for their income. There are areas of Merseyside, in other words, where it is an understatement to speak of massive unemployment: unemployment has become as normal as work.

A further breakdown by duration adds to the picture. The official statistics, and especially national figures, include a large element of transients, voluntary and involuntary job-changers on the register for a relatively short time. In Liverpool, at the beginning of 1980, 40 per cent. of those on the register had been unemployed for *more than a year*, compared to 26 per cent. nationally. This clearly has important implications for the individual and the community. In the past, long-term unemployment in Liverpool may have been attributed to an unusually large hard core of unskilled workers, unadapted to work or workshy. While there is some evidence that a hard core exists, it can only account for a small fraction of the long-term unemployed. Liverpool nevertheless has a disproportionate number of unskilled workers. The fact that in mid-1980 the ratio of general labourers to vacancies on the register of local Employment Offices was 283 : 1 compared to a national average of 33 : 1 gives some indication of the character of the labour force and local problems. But other categories also came off badly : a ratio of 10 : 1 for craft occupations (2 : 1 nationally) and a ratio of 12 : 1 for clerical occupations (6 : 1 nationally). If you want numbers rather than percentages, to see the size of the problem, in September 1980 the Employment Offices had some 48,000 clients looking for work and 1,000 vacancies to offer.

Bleak Times for Youth

The incidence of juvenile unemployment locally is masked in much the same way by national figures about unemployed youngsters. The level in Merseyside is again higher than elsewhere, the concentration greater and the prospects bleaker. As unemployment continues to rise, the figures I quote, necessarily dated, once more understate the problem—terrible though they are. The Planning Office calculated Liverpool rates of 36 per cent. for those under 18 and 32 per cent. for the 18–19 age group a year ago. In certain districts the rates are much higher and it is here that the most serious special problems arise. I will return below to these.

Of the summer 1980 school-leavers in Merseyside as a whole something like a third went on to further education or found employment in a reasonable time, another third joined youth opportunity schemes, while the rest remained entirely unemployed. With thousands of youngsters chasing literally a handful of jobs then, and the economic situation worsening since, they have no chance. Actual numbers may give a more realistic picture. In September 1980 5,700 young people were registered with the Careers Offices in Liverpool as seeking work. The figure fluctuates, of course, peaking at the end of the school year, declining as summer-leavers find jobs or are absorbed by youth opportunity programmes. September 10 years earlier, however, the number was only 1,300—a measure of Liverpool's deteriorating economy (while the Careers Service may have been less well organised then to reach all school-leavers, the total population was larger). Among those unemployed in September 1980 were some 900 who had left school in summer 1979 and almost 3,000 of the 5,300 who left in summer 1980. These figures show the

20

high proportion of young people who cannot move directly from school to work (*i.e.* experience rejection in the labour market) and the significant proportion who have been unemployed for more than a year. In addition to those on the books of the Careers Service, there were some 2,500 under the age of 19 registered with the Employment Offices. These figures hide the true scale of shortfall in job opportunities because there were also some 4,200 youngsters on youth programmes of one sort or another. The other side of the coin is even more dramatic: the number of vacancies notified to the Careers Service was 12 in July, when school-leavers hit the streets, and has fallen as low as four. Of course, many youngsters compete for vacancies with adults in the Jobcentres and many find work by approaching employers directly—but the message here is no different. Firms report hundreds of applications for a single post and youngsters report almost as many unsuccessful letters or visits. While lack of qualifications may sometimes be a factor (of which more below), one Merseyside factory had 1,500 suitably qualified applicants for 50 apprenticeships.

The problem, again, has structural causes. In addition to the general decline in workplaces noted earlier, there seems to be a decline in job opportunities for the young. Cost-conscious firms have been reducing the number of young people taken on as trainees (and the number of apprenticeships in Liverpool has always been very low compared to other parts of the country) because of pessimistic assumptions about the future. They have also cut the number of school-leavers taken on for unskilled work and for odd jobs around the factory or office. Cost-cutting apart, some of the jobs that were suitable for such youngsters are probably disappearing as the result of technological developments. In other sectors, unions seem to have forced juvenile wages relatively high compared to adults, so that it hardly pays an employer to take on a young person when he can employ an experienced worker for little more. Public sector cutbacks, on the other hand, have reduced the number of outlets for O-level leavers.

Many of the unemployed youngsters live in inner-city districts with their accumulation of problems. It is often said that from the mid-1960s to the mid-1970s the heart was torn out of Liverpool. People were moved out by the local authorities, often against their own desires, as part of slum clearance policies. Many of the better paid (*i.e.* skilled or semi-skilled) workers also moved out with their families. One way or another, the inner-city population was halved, leaving behind those least able to cope and poor accommodation

21

that was filled by the disadvantaged of one sort or another. These areas are generally depressing beyond belief. Housing standards are bad and accommodation is overcrowded; there are few amenities; the environment is inhospitable; 15 per cent. of the land is actually vacant or derelict; apartment blocks (never designed for living, it is true) have been vandalised beyond repair, boarded up or torn down —all adding to the atmosphere of decay. Other indicators of malaise are just as bad: poor health, low educational achievement, low incomes, high crime rates, many problem families and, of course, massive unemployment. Inner-city disasters are matched, however, in some of the newer outer-city estates. In Kirkby there are streets in which the shop-fronts are permanently boarded up, even in daytime, and where one house in seven has been vandalised: the visiting Southerner might think he was in parts of New York rather than Britain. Youngsters from these areas obviously enter the labour market with many handicaps. Among these is the image potential employers have of the district and its residents. " Liverpool 8 need not apply ", a phrase that made the rounds some years ago, sums it up.

Some figures again, this time on educational achievements. Half of those registered as unemployed with the Liverpool Careers Offices in October 1979 had no qualifications whatsoever and a further 20 per cent. only had CSE at grades 4/5—thus 70 per cent. did not reach the level required for craft apprenticeships. The picture is not much different for school-leavers as a whole in certain districts. Examination results are so far below the national averages that the gap is almost as wide as between Britain and some Third World states. One survey, a couple of years ago, found that only 3·5 per cent. had five or more O-levels compared to 22 per cent. in the North-West as a whole (a comparison which again shows how the regional tables that are usually published disguise the Liverpool reality from readers elsewhere). The great majority of children leave school at the earliest possible moment. Basic skills (the three Rs) are poor in many areas and there are areas which produce not a single school-leaver able to win a grant for higher education.

To some extent, their poor educational record makes such young people particularly vulnerable to unemployment. As we have seen, there is already a large pool of unskilled labour seeking work while, on the whole, such workplaces seem to be on the decline—yet it is to such work that low achievers are generally restricted. A survey of the Vauxhall area of Liverpool was undertaken some years ago. This is an area of multiple deprivation. A high proportion of the residents are unskilled or semi-skilled workers, incomes are low, unemployment high, and the environment as described earlier. School-leavers are set to follow their parents' footsteps : some 80 per cent. of the group went into unskilled or semi-skilled work—two or three times the national average. While the absence of better work in the area was an important factor, their lack of qualifications would have barred them in any case.

Though the inner-city areas contain a disproportionate number of children born with handicaps of one sort or another, the effect of this is marginal in relation to the figures quoted above and their poor achievements cannot be ascribed to lower natural abilities (the cycle of deprivation theory). Nor, really, can they be explained entirely by poor educational facilities, poorer though these are than in middle-class areas despite LEA attempts to inject extra resources into priority areas. The negative attitude of children to school goes some way to explaining their record. Partly because their families live in overcrowded tenements without play space at home, children play in the streets from an early age and develop strong peer-group cultures hostile to school, reflected in high truancy rates or, at best, switched-off attendance. Unlike the children of the " established " working class, encouraged by their parents to see career prospects in education or at least taught to see school as an inescapable fact of life, the children here opt out wherever possible. Yet another study of a downtown area (disguised as Roundhouse) notes the way in which children of six and seven years are already socialised into a sub-culture which makes it psychologically difficult for them to take advantage of educational and other opportunities that occur thereafter.

One explanation of low achievement, therefore, is that school is marginal to the lives of such youngsters. Their attitude can be seen in another light, however. The Vauxhall survey suggested that they switched off from school because they quite realistically saw it as a waste of time. Their horizons were not necessarily as limited as their subsequent careers suggest. Many boys would have liked industrial apprenticeships and girls also mentioned jobs that actually required some qualifications. A more recent study in the Granby area showed that many hoped to find more rewarding jobs at a future stage in their lives and were not really aware of the trap in which they were caught. The absence of parental experience or local job opportunities, however, removes any practical reinforcement for such dreams.

It is wrong, nevertheless, to attach too much weight to the educational factor in explaining the high rate of juvenile unemployment. True, some young people appear almost unemployable to many employers, either because of their apparent illiteracy or because of their dress and manner. Much effort is currently put by the Manpower Services Commission and FE colleges into teaching them " life skills ", meaning how to apply for a job, and there is some evidence that such instruction can be effective. Young people do get jobs as a result and, to their surprise, employers often find a heart of gold beneath the rough exterior : workers as useful as those of more orthodox appearance, even as pleasant. They also find that some of the jobs for which they usually demand school qualifications can be done quite as well without (O-level requirements are too often just a way of shortening the queue of applicants). But none of this makes more jobs available. There is no evidence that employers take on more young people because applicants are better prepared. To that extent, the whole campaign to make young people more " employable " is irrelevant to the underlying, structural causes of juvenile unemployment and runs the risk of misleading those concerned with youth programmes.

Having made this point, let me immediately stress that the teaching of life skills is not irrelevant as far as individual youngsters are concerned. Juvenile unemployment rates, high though they are, mask even more serious problems for particular groups : those who because of poor school records, personal characteristics or even the wrong address, find it hardest to impress employers. The longer they are unemployed, the harder they find it. Employers often prefer the recent school-leaver to youngsters who have been without work for any length of time, suspecting that the latter are unemployable. There may even be some truth in this as youngsters develop " undesirable " attitudes or their spirit is simply undermined. While courses do not increase the number of vacancies, they may give those at the bottom of the pile a better chance of getting one of the available jobs, distributing employment and unemployment more evenly among the age group and thus breaking the vicious circle which leads to a hard core of permanently unemployed.

Time Bomb of Unemployment?

A few years ago, in the early days of the Job Creation Programme, a dinner was held in Liverpool for the chairmen of area boards from throughout the country and as the local chairman I was called on for some after-dinner words. I warned of the effects of unemployment on the young, particularly of the social and political consequences of disaffection. " Ridley's rivers of blood speech ", as it came to be known, apparently caused much offence among the more conservative participants. Shortly after, however, in 1978, my fears became respectable. Peter Walker said in a Commons debate that we were entering a phase in which a whole crowd of young people were becoming hostile to society.

He saw two consequences of extensive and extended juvenile unemployment. The first was that while young people were not yet organised by the criminal network, they would be if the current situation continued. The crime wave is already with us, even if not organised. Crime is the only booming industry in Merseyside. I have referred to vandalism. This is not just a matter of smashed lamp-posts and graffiti but of the systematic destruction of housing and other social facilities by young people. Not that they see this as a crime, and indeed there is no profit in it for them : it is simply a way of passing the time. Juvenile crime figures are alarming for all that. Something like a quarter of all prosecutions by the Merseyside police involve children under 16 and another quarter of young people between 16 and 21. Though prosecutions run high, moreover, they are only the tip of the iceberg as only a small proportion of offenders are ever caught.

Crime cannot be directly attributed to unemployment. The crime rate, though gradually increasing, was high before the present crisis and many of the offenders are still of school age in any case (around 40 per cent. of those caught stealing, because one must add in the juveniles cautioned by the police on their first offence and not prosecuted). But under-16 crime is particularly high in those districts where unemployment is also high and the latter is inseparable from the environment of social malaise in which crime becomes part of the normal way of life. The great majority of juveniles of working age that appear in the courts, moreover, and the majority of adults, appear to be unemployed. In the words of one 19-year-old : " people can't get jobs and the dole money is useless and so people take to robbing; it's as simple as that ". It isn't as simple, of course, but enforced idleness is doubtless a factor, as is the feeling of exclusion from work. A recent report of the Merseyside Probation Service showed that 80 per cent. of its clientele had no jobs. It noted that the boredom and frustration of unemployment could lead to anti-social behaviour and, more serious, that anti-social attitudes could harden as unemployable ex-offenders came to feel unwanted and outside the mainstream of society.

Peter Walker's second point was that political forces, including the National Front and extreme left-wing revolutionary organisations, were taking full advantage of unemployment. Whether exclusion from work and rejection by organised society, for that is how it is often seen, will also lead to serious political alienation is another matter. Some would argue that there is already considerable alienation among inner-city populations and that unemployment is only one of the many factors involved. Positive attachment to our institutions is probably not as high as our politicians like to think anywhere in Britain, but cynicism about the system and those that operate it may be especially high in Liverpool. The structure of local party politics may have as much to do with this as social malaise (hence the astonishing success of Liberals in mobilising an anti-establishment vote at local elections). More to the point, however, is that a recent survey of young people in Liverpool 8 found that 85 per cent. of those interviewed had no political convictions at all; many were vehement in their indifference to politics. Half the group were even unwilling to define themselves as members of the working (or any other) class—hardly fertile soil for extremist movements of the Left.

What we may have among the disadvantaged inner-city young, in other words, is passive alienation. They have opted out of the polity if, indeed, they were ever socialised into it in the first place. There is no sign yet of significant political activity among the young directed against the existing order. Opinions differ about the extent to which alienated youngsters form a pool that could be mobilised by political activists. Conservatives and social democrats may fear it, the far Left may hope for it, but I have my doubts. The intellectual demands revolutionary movements make on their members (reading news-sheets, etc.) and the commitments of time they demand (selling news-sheets, etc.) are probably too high. The National Front is another matter, because it offers a rather different outlet for frustrated energies. Street fights are more likely to strike a chord than organised political action. But it is well to remember that riots can be triggered off by all sorts of organisations or, indeed, by no organisations at all. There, perhaps, lies the real danger. A generation idle and frustrated because unemployed; rejected by employers, thus alienated; concentrated in certain districts where the environment itself is grim—not revolution, but simple undirected violence and pointless destruction.

As Harold Macmillan pointed out in his recent TV interview, the costs of unemployment outweigh whatever eventual benefits the present Government may see, either in the gradual dampening of inflation or in the gradual restructuring of British industry. The loss of production nationally cannot be offset in a few years: by then we will have further weakened our competitive position in world trade and thus marched further along the road of deindustrialisation. Even if the economy did revive, the wasted years could never be offset for the individual by subsequent employment. This is particularly true of the school-leaver. Some will never fulfil their work potential because of the absence of opportunities to develop skills in their formative years. Some will be psychologically affected by their apparent rejection by society: though the adult unemployed may experience greater financial hardship, it is for the juvenile that the experience is likely to be most traumatic, because he is at the most vulnerable age emotionally. Many will doubtless settle later into normal patterns of work and life, but some will remain permanently scarred. If that is not a time-bomb already set, it is a bomb whose fuse may be lit in some future crisis.

Meanwhile, we all have to pay the costs of unemployment, direct and indirect. Enlightened self-interest, if nothing else, should convince us that juvenile unemployment costs us more than we can ever hope to recoup if and when Thatcherite policies succeed. A permanently depressed Merseyside will also remain a financial charge on a revived economy. The unconservative disciples of *laissez-faire* who have taken over the Conservative Party may dismiss humanitarian policies as a form of " do-goodism " that only harm the economy— but they are bad book-keepers. They may dismiss economic planning as distortion of the economy—but that, too, is bad book-keeping.

When I was a student of political science, and Sir Ivor Jennings was the textbook we read, the case made for stable one-party government with strong leadership was that it enabled a government to implement its policies. We could then judge its success or failure. The phrase, I remember, was that a government should be given a rope long enough to hang itself. Unlike Mrs. Thatcher, I am against capital punishment. But I am coming round to it.

27

ECONOMIC ASPECTS OF UNEMPLOYMENT

MAURICE PESTON

IT is well known that Beveridge in *Full Employment in a Free Society* regarded an average unemployment rate of 3 per cent. as full employment. Keynes agreed with that, although he thought it erred somewhat on the side of hope rather than reality. Other economists such as Paish and Meade, defining full employment as the maximum level of employment compatible with price stability, recommended an unemployment percentage of 4 per cent.

Ten years later by the end of the 1950s Paish had changed his estimates, and said that the non-inflationary unemployment percentage was something between 2 per cent. and 2·5 per cent. of the labour force. He appeared still to stick to this figure 10 years later, and was branded as a right-wing reactionary for so doing. By contrast, in 1967 I, in one of my more extravagant moods, was writing: " With benefits at their present level the deliberate creation of unemployment much above 1·5 per cent. for any significant period of time is quite intolerable ".

Now, some of these numerical differences may be due to which set of unemployment figures various economists look at and whether they are referring to an average around which unemployment fluctuates or to a maximum. But what is most striking today about the debate on policy before 1967 is the tiny numerical gap between the so-called progressives and reactionaries, and the extraordinary optimism that they all shared. And, of course, this optimism was warranted. In 1951 there were just over 200,000 people unemployed equal to about 1·0 per cent. of all employees. In 1966 the comparable figures were 280,000, *i.e.* 1·2 per cent. Even in such a bad year as 1963, we are not talking about more than half a million unemployed, implying a rate of 2·2 per cent. Perhaps an even better way of appreciating the point is not to examine unemployment but employment. In 1950 the employed labour force was 23·3m. people. This rose by more than two millions to 25·4m. in 1966. (The comparable figures for employees only is even more impressive—a rise of two and a half million from 20·8m. to 23·3m.) In other words, for about two decades the economy showed a remarkable capacity to accom-

---

* The author is Professor of Economics, Queen Mary College, University of London.

modate a rising working population. In 1967 the employed labour force fell to 25m. and was at the same figure in 1979. Employment ranged from 24·4m. to 25·1m., and essentially what appears to have happened in the past dozen or so years is that our ability to create a great many net new jobs has disappeared.

In trying to understand what has happened, the next point to appreciate is the way the increase in unemployment has occurred in a series of bursts. There have been four such powerful upward movements, in 1967, 1971, 1975–1976, and 1980, the last not yet being finished. To be set against them there has only been one year of reversal of comparable size, Mr. Barber's boom year of 1973. Unemployment has moved forward as if on a ratchet, gaining even higher levels which fall only a little. Of the years since 1966, unemployment has risen on nine occasions and fallen on five, with the absolute magnitude of the former far exceeding that of the latter. The economy has followed a four-year cycle, but the duration and scale of the downswings have exceeded those of the upswings. Indeed, in 15 years unemployment has never fallen for more than two successive years. (For that matter only once in the past three decades has unemployment fallen three years in a row.) I return to this consideration when I come to consider the outlook for the rest of the decade and the possibilities for policy.

The Structure of Unemployment

Before doing that, however, attention must also be paid to the structure of unemployment. In 1966, for example, about a quarter of the unemployed were in the under-25 age group. Nowadays the figure is nearer to a half, although these young people comprise only a fifth of the working population. Almost all facets of the unemployment experience show its effects on young people to have been worse for them than the population at large, with the groups most affected being the youngest men, and all young women. This last point is of more general significance. Of the employed population in 1979 (about) 60 per cent. were men and 40 per cent. women. This compares with 70 per cent. and 30 per cent. respectively in 1951. It should be added, however, that the male and female trends are not strictly comparable. The former represents a decline in the number of men employed full time in production industries; the latter comprises to a large extent an expansion of women working part time in the service (and chiefly the public) sector. Moreover, in the 1950s and 1960s registered male unemployment rose as a fraction of the total so that in 1971, for example, nine-tenths of all the registered unemployed were men. Since then the fraction of females unemployed has risen so that they now comprise some 30 per cent. of the total (about the same as in 1960). It is worth adding that the total number of people registered as unemployed does not include all those who were in work or would take a job if it were offered to them. About 10 per cent. of unemployed men do not register as such, and, perhaps, as many as 50 per cent. unemployed married women also still see no point in registering.

Turning now to causes, it is vital to understand that the stock of unemployed is a continually changing one. Unemployment is a dynamic phenomenon, being the residual of those coming on to the register and those coming off it. It rises if the number going on to the register exceeds the number coming off, or if the average period of time spent on the register goes up. The upwards trend we have been talking about results from both forces. It is specially worth noting that in the early 1950s, of the stock of unemployed, only some 30,000 had been out of work for a year or more, and quite a few of those would have been on the margin of employability. Today, the figure for long-term unemployed is getting on for 400,000, and is still going up.

Reverting to the dynamics, in the three years from the beginning of 1977 to the end of 1979, some 270–290,000 people either joined or left the unemployment register every month. The net flow on to the register varied from about minus 20,000 to plus 15,000 people per month. This was, therefore, a time of slowly rising or slowly falling unemployment. In 1980, the number coming on to the register had risen towards 320,000, and the number going off had dropped to about 260,000. The result is that the net monthly flow has built up to about 60,000. This would mean, if it became the characteristic position, that over 700,000 people would be added to the register in a year.

There is one other factual consideration that needs to be considered as a background to a discussion of causation. The United Kingdom is not alone in experiencing what appears to be a chronic rise in unemployment. Most of the advanced industrialised countries have experienced it, but not to the same degree. Again, in most of them youth unemployment is higher than average, so some of the causal factors must be common to all countries. Countries do, however, differ in both the level and the rate of change of unemployment, so that there are specific, national causal factors to look for as well. In particular, the United Kingdom appears to have moved from a below average to an average and now to an above average percentage of the labour force out of work. (In the 1970s our inflation experience, too, was worse than average for the advanced industrial countries. All in all, United Kingdom economic performance and economic policy-making was as bad as any country and inferior to most in that decade.) No one doubts that the central cause of the problem is a fall in demand for final output relative to capacity. This is partly a matter of the typical shocks that hit a mixed economy and its automatic reaction to them. Waves of optimism and pessimism on the part of both firms and households cause economic fluctuations, and even with the best possible policy response will continue to do so.

Explanation

Connected with this explanation that unemployment is linked to deficient demand in general is the important point that part of the demand deficiency will be for new capital goods. This means that when demand starts to rise again capacity will be insufficient, so that bottlenecks will occur sooner. (A related phenomenon is the decline in the investment in human capital, notably in apprenticeships. Shortages of trained manpower will also inhibit expansion in future). The result will be some domestically generated inflation, and the balance-of-payments constraint may also be brought into play at an earlier stage. And to the extent that workers have succeeded in raising real wages excessively, and the additional costs of hiring labour have also gone up, what capital investment does occur will be labour saving. These factors may also be strengthened by the very expectations that they will be even more significant in future. Firms may not take on labour or add sufficiently to their capital stock because they may not believe the demand for output will be sustained. What machines they buy will use as little labour as possible, because of expectations about rising wage costs. Finally, the Government may become convinced that expansionary macroeconomic policy will fail, and firms respond by raising prices rather than output and employment. The paradox is, of course, that it may have been an original failure on the part of the Government to maintain full employment that created the problem in the first place. Certainly, it is hard to reject the view that government worries about both inflation and the trade balance have been contractionary in effect and have also made any subsequent expansion more difficult. This is true to a considerable extent of each of the four bursts of unemployment we have already examined.

Oil Cost Push

Of course, the major shock to have hit the world in recent times was the oil price rise of the early 1970s. Although the real transfer of resources to the O.P.E.C. countries was eroded by subsequent inflation they have done all they can by raising prices to keep their original advantage. The effect of the rise in the price of oil was contractionary because the initial transfer of funds to the oil producers could not be spent immediately. Most oil consumers, feeling poorer, spent less, but the oil producers took time to spend more. In addition, to avoid the consequences of the oil price rise, many countries introduced fiscal and monetary policies aimed to cut demand even more. One country that failed to do so for quite a while was the United States, and, despite the benefit this gave to the rest of the advanced world, she herself has suffered accordingly. The United Kingdom, too, reacted slowly, and had a much more inflationary experience than most of her competitors.

There can be little doubt that oil cost push has built an inflationary bias into most people's expectations. All parts of society, but certainly the trades unions, are much more sensitive about inflation than they were 20 years ago. The result has been the vicious circle we have already remarked on. But it is probable that increased concern with real income, and unwillingness to accept a reduction in its rate of increase, let alone level, preceded the oil price rise, and helps to explain the upward movement of both inflation and unemployment in the late 1960s.

It should be recalled that, although Keynes did not regard a rise in the real wage as a *cause* of unemployment, he did accept that it was an *effect*. Workers would resist a reduction in the money wage as a method of restoring full employment; but they would not resist a reduction in the real wage, if there was a rise in the price level as a result of expansionary macroeconomic policy. Now, the behaviour of the real wage over the cycle remains a controversial matter in economics, but Keynesian theory and policy certainly forbid real wage resistance in the upswing. To put the point positively, if money wages accelerate as nominal demand is expanded, the main effect of policy will be to add to inflation. The more money wages accelerate, the smaller the magnitude of the upswing. The more they are expected to accelerate, the less likely firms are to take on workers. The more the Government believe this will happen, the less likely they are to initiate the upswing in the first place. It is arguable, therefore, that the tendency for unemployment to become higher in booms and slumps in the 1960s resulted from expansionary policies having a greater positive effect on money wage increases (and contractionary policies having a smaller negative effect). Rises in demand were less effective in creating employment and were brought to a stop earlier. Falls in demand cut output more and wages and prices less. It follows that the unemployment problem of the 1970s would have emerged without O.P.E.C. What the oil producers did was worsen a trend that was already there.

Other Trends

There are, however, some other trend factors that need to be mentioned. One is the rise in unemployment benefit relative to after-tax incomes, and especially the so-called earnings related supplement. Changing the regulations for married women has also caused more of them to register when they lose a job, although as I have already stated, only about half of the number of women who are unemployed do in fact register, so that in this way the current figure is a truer estimate of unemployment than used to be the case. Many attempts have been made to estimate the significance of this, the range of adjustment to the unemployment figures being put somewhere between 0·25 per cent. and 1·25 per cent. A second is the effect of the employers' national insurance contributions and related costs of hiring and firing workers, which will act as a disincentive to take on staff, especially if a sustained expansion of demand is not expected. A third is the effect of the increase of incomes on the search for new jobs, and a willingness to take what is offered. This is particularly interesting from a theoretical standpoint. The evidence is that unemployment does not result from workers quitting jobs voluntarily to look for new ones. It may be, however, that once they are fired they are less anxious to seek new employment or accept what is being offered to them. This may partly be because of the rise in various social security payments. My own conclusion is that, while these trend factors are of technical interest, they are not really important. Of the two million-plus workers registered as unemployed at the moment I would suggest that at most 300,000 could come into the category of being more or less voluntarily unemployed. I therefore think that an appropriate definition of full employment would give rise to a figure somewhere in the range of 600,000 to 750,000 unemployed. While I would veer towards the lower figure, as will be seen, the prospects for the next decade are so poor that there is no need whatsoever to argue between the two extremes. I might add that there are those, out of malice or ignorance, who try to show that the majority of the unemployed are voluntarily unemployed. If by all the unemployed we mean those who were in jobs, and those who want jobs, if anything the published figures are an under-estimate, not an overestimate.

The Prospects

Let me, therefore, consider finally the prospects for employment up to the end of the 1980s. I shall concentrate on the unemployment figures seasonally adjusted (ignoring school-leavers). This is the reason why the numbers will appear lower than those in the news-paper headlines, and why in my terms the two million mark has not yet been passed. Concentrating on mid-year figures and, there-fore, regarding the representative figure for 1980 as 1·7m., my own forecast is that the figure for 1981 will be 2·1m. I also believe that on unchanged policies, unemployment will go on rising until mid-1982 but at a slightly slower rate, leading to a figure then of 2·4m. This means that the numbers actually unemployed, as reported in the Press, could well touch 3·0m. at some time. This forecast is fairly conservative; there are economists who are projecting a much larger figure.

What also has to be borne in mind in considering policy is the increase in the number of people entering the labour force in this period. This is largely a demographic matter, but there is also the trend in labour force participation to take into account. Current estimates are that something between 70,000 and 140,000 new jobs will have to be created each year just to allow for the greater number of those available for work. To keep the numbers down, let us assume that something near the bottom of the range is the correct number. Let us also assume that the Government's economic policy shifts immediately to an expansionary mode. We know from past experience that the impact on unemployment will be delayed for a year, so that even with instantaneous action, the forecast of 2·1m. will hold for 1981. Suppose that it was thought desirable to get that down to 1m. by 1990. Recall that this is well above what I would define as full employment, and I doubt very much whether many other economists would disagree. The task for policy would then be to knock 1·1m. off the unemployment figures in nine years, *i.e.* 120,000 per annum. This would mean creating altogether 200,000 net new jobs every year for the whole of that period.

If we consider the past 15 years, in only one year, as we have noted, that of the ill-fated Barber boom, has unemployment fallen by over 200,000. In no other year has it fallen by as much as 100,000.

We have had experience of rapid job expansion, of course. My opening sentences reminded us of the great increase in employment in the 1950s and the first half of the 1960s, while unemployment varied very little, at least by present-day standards. That really was an era of full employment, with output growing at a trend rate above 2·5 per cent. per annum. (It is also worth recalling how critical commentators were of our economic performance at that time.) The question we now have to ask is: is it conceivable that starting from the existing position we could actually beat the job-creation performance of the 1950s? Could we in nine years increase employment by 1·8m.? The Manpower Services Commission in 1977 did appear to believe that sufficiently rapid job creation was possible. I think they were over-optimistic then, and there are many more grounds for pessimism now. One is the world recession coupled with a likely slower underlying rate of growth of world trade. A second is inflation, which inhibits policy and the positive response to policy in the ways we have already suggested. In particular, in the 1950s and early 1960s, expansion was believed in and was relied on by businessmen. It is not believed in now, and certainly not relied on.

Single-figure inflation is just about possible some time in 1981, and quite likely in 1982. This is the outcome of the depression created by the Government's policies. There is nothing to suggest that the Government has actually done anything to solve the real inflation problem, so that expansion in employment after 1982 if it occurs at all rapidly would get the country back to two-digit inflation without much delay.

Then there is the vexed question of the new technology and labour productivity. It is argued that the trend rise in unemployment since the 1960s is attributable to a considerable extent to labour-saving technology. More to the point it is being suggested that output can now expand even more easily without undue pressure on the labour market. This is not just a matter of the new technology, but also because of our inefficiency with the old technology which firms are increasingly trying to overcome. We are so inefficient now in many lines of production that even getting to the average performance of our competitors (let alone the best) would comprise a technical revolution. In recent years much of the employment expansion we have tried has been in the public sector. If policy is so constrained that this level of employment is not even maintained but is actually decreased, the task for the private sector is increased pro rata.

I infer from this that, if we had an expansionary policy initiated

35

by the present Government, on the most optimistic assumptions (actually ludicrously optimistic), it might create 900,000 to 1m. new jobs in nine years. This would mean that by 1990, the numbers unemployed would be something like 1·8 to 2·0 million. We would have done little more than accommodate the rising potential labour force. But the Government will not make a U-turn immediately, and may not start much in the way of expansion even later in 1981. Moreover, there will be another world recession before the decade is over. The realistic outlook is, therefore, poorer still.

Is There an Alternative?

Could a different policy do better? Although my answer to this question is yes, it is a measure of the mess we are in that with the best will in the world it is hard to believe that unemployment could be got down to one million by 1990. Suppose the trades unions co-operated with a really tight incomes policy, which means that for a year or so (but no longer) average real incomes would also be constrained. At the same time let public expenditure and public sector employment be allowed to rise in real terms. Thirdly, postulate some tax cuts, notably in the employer's national insurance contribution. Lastly, postulate an active manpower policy of retraining, education for leisure, earlier retirement, and modifications of the working year with corresponding wage adjustments. (I do not believe that there is much need to ease the restraint in the nominal money supply or devalue sterling, since the required real effects would be achieved by the incomes policy. Monetary ease and devaluation would only be necessary if the incomes policy failed; but then, in my opinion, the complete strategy would collapse.) Even with this scenario working perfectly, and assuming some modest improvement in our technical performance, at most I could envisage the addition of some 140,000 to 150,000 new jobs per annum for the whole period, making rather more than a million and a third overall. This would imply a reduction in the number of unemployed by (say) 500,000, leaving a figure of 1·5 million in 1990. It would then take at least the first five years of the 1990s before we achieved full employment.

Moreover, given the behaviour of the trades unions in 1978, this version of events is also optimistic to the point of naïvete. After all, in 1978 the foundation had been laid for a comparatively non-inflationary economic advance. From that starting-point full employment might well have been attained by 1985, with increases in both the public and private sectors. But the winter of discontent destroyed all that, with public sector workers second to none in their rush to disaster.

Why would things be different on yet another attempt? The only answer must lie in the rationality that stems from considering the alternative. The one benefit of the present Government's policies is that they make a mainstream economic strategy look so much more sensible. Perhaps workers, their leaders and employers, will learn the lesson. But even then, the point must be reiterated, the employment outlook except in the very long term would merely be less bad rather than good. By the 1990s we will have had two decades of less than full employment. We will have done major damage to a lot of people's lives, notably young people's. Even vigorous action now (and setting doctrinaire prejudices to one side) will not restore anything like satisfactory conditions for the current generation for quite a long time. Postponement of a new policy adds to the damage, and increases the danger that this scale of unemployment will start to be regarded as normal, even inevitable. What the social and political consequences of that will be is for others to say, but it is hard to believe that they will be desirable.

POLITICAL ASPECTS OF UNEMPLOYMENT: THE ALTERNATIVE POLICY

AUSTIN MITCHELL

CENTRAL to the increasingly desperate Tory assertion that " there is no alternative " is a belief that Britain's situation has changed so drastically that other economic strategies are outdated. Only Thatcherism will work. Yet to the more sceptical, though Britain's problems may be more acute they are still basically the same. One law certainly applies. Governments which pursue policies calculated to produce unemployment get it, and on an increasing scale.

The new economics is a revival of the orthodoxies of the 1920s and today's situation is much the same as that then facing Keynes: mass unemployment caused by deficient demand. Demand was first savaged by the massive transfer of surpluses and purchasing power to OPEC. Keynesian remedies then appeared to fail because, with a large budget deficit caused by the depression itself, government was afraid to increase it further. Raging inflation and the danger to the balance of payments made it fear demand expansion even more, so a new orthodoxy was installed: cuts, deflation, monetarism, finally Thatcherism. By cutting demand still further and eliminating our competitiveness the underlying situation was made far worse. It set us on the road now leading to three million unemployed, from which the only way out is not a U-turn, which would be a non-U-turn from the present Prime Minister, but a complete break with deflationary economics.

The Economics of Thatcherism

Deflationary strategies are the cause of much of our increasing unemployment. They are also the obstacle to any attempt to get unemployment back to 500,000 by demand expansion. Thatcherism, the latest and most dangerous deflation, is an unholy trinity of three brands of medicine. First is a determined attack on public spending to cut P.S.B.R., prevent " crowding out " and stimulate activity through tax cuts. The justifications are doubtful. Recession and unemployment increase borrowing: competition for resources means

---

* The author is Labour Member of Parliament for Grimsby.

little when they are massively under-employed; tax cuts generate less activity than increased spending. So the real effect is to depress the economy, reduce consumer demand and force industry to borrow more.

The second medicine is control of the money supply, arbitrarily defined as sterling M3, though other measures point in different directions. Monetarists regard the volume of money, alone among economic phenomena, as determined by supply not demand. Yet money is endogenous not exogenous. So when Mrs. Thatcher says she will not " print money " she means she might. Demand generates printing. Since the Conservatives will not control money directly they must ration it by interest rates, high ones, depressing the economy to suit a lower money supply. This is merely an exaggeration of the whole disastrous pattern of British economic policy: management by deflation. Like past deflations this hits our internationally traded sector which has always been robbed of the steady growth and the opportunity to break through to the economies of scale its competitors have reached. Yet past deflations have been invoked because of a threat to sterling. This excuse is now lacking. Deflation is now being used for doctrinaire reasons, just at the time when North Sea oil provides us with our first chance to grow.

Oil creates a new danger: an overvalued pound. This is the third strategy. High interest rates make a petro-pound doubly attractive. Money comes in, pushes up the pound and increases the money supply which then requires a further increase in interest rates which makes the pound even more attractive. This ratchet effect has now made the pound 19 per cent. higher than in May 1979, 33 per cent. up on the fourth quarter of 1976. Yet the rise is not the real measure of overvaluation, for the pound should have gone down to compensate for high domestic inflation and competitive devaluations, of other currencies such as the dollar, the yen, and now the mark. The resulting overvaluation is massive: a loss of competitiveness of 30 per cent. over the last year and an overvaluation of over 45 per cent. on 1976.

Is this accidental or an essential part of Thatcherism? The rising pound is that transmission mechanism on which Friedman is so vague. Control of the money supply can hardly reduce internal costs. Indeed, deflation and declining production guarantee that unit costs will go up. High interest rates add to them. So monetarism has to work by reducing the price of imports, *vide* Mrs. Thatcher's famous advice to Austin and Pickersgill to " reduce costs by importing more components ". More important, the rising pound is a wall against which industry can be squeezed to complete the process, begun by internal deflation, of forcing cost cuts, squeezing margins and compelling a tough line against labour.

This strategy is not new. It was described by Keynes in *The Economic Consequences of Mr. Churchill* when Winston's misguided return to an overvalued gold standard in 1925 forced industry to restore competitiveness by cutting wages. It failed then. It will fail now. The escape then was devaluation as Britain left the gold standard. The same route offers now.

The Rise of Thatcherism

Tight control of the money supply could directly check inflation by delivering such a blow to the economy that wage push inflation was broken because the power of labour was smashed and demand pull stopped because demand was slashed. To achieve this regeneration of the J curve the blow would have to be massive. Finance is more important in newspaper economics sections than industry and the " independent " commentators and pundits who have usurped the monarchial right to be consulted, to encourage, and to warn, did nothing but encourage as monetarism moved from atavism to orthodoxy. Peter Jay and Samuel Brittan were enthusiastic converts. The popular press took up monetarism without understanding it because it accorded with its own anti-tax, anti-government, anti-union prejudices. The *Financial Times*, *The Times* and both *Telegraphs* preached it. Even the more independent *Observer* and *Guardian* flirted timidly. The latter's economic writers were closet monetarists and Peter Jenkins had come to the simple belief that an alternative had to be tried. He did not evaluate it. The former's William Keegan failed to voice in his flip column the warnings he uttered in *Who Runs the Economy?* So the media totally failed in their duty to inform and to explain, a major betrayal when the wider public neither understood nor accepted the Keynesian techniques which had ensured well-being since the war.

The climate was favourable to Thatcherism because uncertain. Yet the balance of economic forces made its rise remorseless. The interests of finance, making and manipulating money, often differ from those of industry; making things, providing jobs. They diverge on interest rates, exchange rates, growth. So the gap between them becomes a gulf when Thatcherite economics is used to restore money to primacy. Finance, banking, the City and their mouthpiece the Bank of England became enthusiastic converts to doctrines which clothed their prejudices in science, suited their self-interest and promised to restore elected government to that short leash which fixed exchange rates had previously held them on. Sterling M3 is quick to respond to changes in borrowing and easily manipulated. Any overshoot due to high demand for credit automatically generates another as investors lose the taste for gilts, the Government has to turn to the banking system, money supply then rises further and interest rates have to go up to maintain " confidence ". The invisible Government is back in the saddle.

Yet industry, which was to suffer the consequences, remained supine. Finance has won the long historic battle between Britain's two dominant interests. Manipulation of wealth on a world scale has been given priority over the production of wealth. Weakened by the battering of stop-go, undermined by the remorseless rise of imports, losing jobs at a more rapid rate than its overseas competitors, industry grovelled before the rod for its back. Dependence on the market and the City had installed a fifth column of finance men in the boardrooms and upper echelons. Moreover, industry shares a propensity all too common to British interest groups: an obsession with self-appointed opponents so great as to blind to self-interest. This fixation with unions and big government, both of which it blames for its own problems, led to the assumption that a system designed to weaken both must be good for industry. There are strong lobbies for imports, for financial orthodoxy, for international-ism. There is none for growth. The C.B.I. nominally representing industry is so amorphous because of its admission of the banks, the oil companies, the monoliths and multinationals that it repre-sents nothing except a lowest common denominator: a clamour for tax cuts. Thus it welcomed Thatcherism, a system calculated to ruin a large section of its membership.

Yet it was Labour which towed in the Trojan horse. We have always been anxious to prove ourselves respectable. Our practice has been " when in doubt deflate " despite the fact that deflation, trans-ferring purchasing power from borrowers such as industry, govern-ment, house purchasers and consumers to savers, *i.e.* banks, the privately wealthy and the overseas sector is hardly a socialist strategy. A shaky tenure from 1974 and our reaction to the " irresponsible " Barber boom hardened us in the mould. We argued that Keynes was dead, that the spending way was closed. This paved the way for monetarism. Yet we did not even have the excuse that the I.M.F. enforced it. In 1976 that body insisted on export-led growth. It stipulated an exchange rate which would " maintain the competitive position of U.K. manufactures " and targets set not in terms of M3, but of domestic credit expansion. This allows an increase in economic activity due to a surplus in trade without setting off the jangling (and unnecessary) alarm bells M3 triggers. We threw away the opportunity by allowing the Bank of England to stop interest rates from falling even when DCE was contracting. We let the pound rise and spent reserves to support it. We put a floor under it which became a subsidy to speculation, then uncapped it altogether. Money poured into London. The pound rose still more. All this we did to fight inflation. Victory was vital in our weak situation.

To do this made "confidence" crucial, and the Bank's advice dominant over a still Keynesian Treasury. Within months we were fixing, and keeping, M3 targets. The Chancellor had capitulated, not to the theology of monetarism (he called himself a pragmatist), but to its forms and rituals. This put him at the mercy of its priests. Labour often follows financial orthodoxy. Doing so has never previously elicited so little protest. We hurried full employment, economic growth and rising public spending through the ramparts with neither drum nor funeral note. The PLP showed a strange quiescence. Most accepted the Callaghan-Healey "trust us" line without understanding what it implied. Bryan Gould and Jeremy Bray protested at the Finance Group, Bob Sheldon in Treasury, and the Alternative Strategists grumbled loudly. Yet no one rocked the boat through an abandonment of Labour priorities more serious than that of 1976. As the election approached we took pride in the rising pound, symptom of the betrayal.

Making monetarism respectable paved the way for the full-blooded Tory version, a perfect ideology for a party which had ceased to stand for anything beyond " to him that hath ". The end of economic growth had eliminated the easy welfarist assumptions of Macmillanite Toryism. Opting for the Common Market and finance's victory over industry undermined the patriotic assumptions of Chamberlainite Toryism. Heath's failure invalidated expansionism. All that remained were deep instincts: anti-union, anti-government, anti-tax, anti-welfare. Thatcherism fitted these, the moralising propensities of the new Toryism, the class assumptions of supporters who see any economics as a zero-sum game with the working class inconsiderately getting too much, and the anti-state, Poujadist instincts of a small businessman rank and file. So the Tories embraced monetarism with enthusiasm where we had thought we could have the method but not the consequences. Thatcherism was single minded. It eschewed management of the real economy altogether, grossly accelerating inflation, safe in the knowledge that this did not count.

The Economic Consequences of Margaret Thatcher

The result is an impossible outward-bound course for sickly British industry. The internationally traded sector is deliberately squeezed between high interest rates, depressed home markets and crippling exchange rates, to force it to improve productivity and competitiveness. The same pressures will break the unions, and end low productivity, restrictive practices, the propensity to strike. This amounts to supply side tinkering done with a bulldozer. Yet it cannot work because deflation is the enemy of improvement. Businesses need prospects of profitability to invest and grow. Faced with long-term disaster they batten down hatches or go liquid. The result is to entrench Luddism, job protection, overmanning, restrictive practices and the other defensive reflexes which have bedevilled us for so long.

Any one of the three weights festooned round industry's neck would be crippling. Collectively they kill. The decline in consumer demand and the high interest rates have reduced output, pushed up liquidations, bankruptcies and unemployment. We have rushed faster and deeper into depression than any other country, yet as an Oil Power we should suffer least. The economy has begun a rapid wind-down, concealed by massive de-stocking, the failure to invest and survival by borrowing. The " school dinner syndrome " applies in nationalised industries such as steel. Increasing prices due to tighter cash limits and the greedy insistence on using charges as a surrogate taxation reduce demand. This increases unit costs, for even with plant closures remaining plants still operate well below break-even capacity, thus increasing costs and prices still further and allowing competitors to take an increasing share of the market. Meanwhile demand for coal and railways drops, their costs rise. As electricity consumption falls the Central Electricity Generating Board's costs per kilowatt hour increase. The slide is remorseless.

All this will be made worse in the months ahead by over-valuation of sterling. Changes in the exchange rate feed through slowly. Ours are already visible in falling exports where world trade has increased and manufactured imports (as distinct from raw material and fuels which are declining with domestic demand) holding steady in a declining consumer market. The subsidy overvaluation provided to imports and the levy it imposes on exports will come as the last and worst blow from Thatcherism. Overvaluation closes Conservative escape routes. Cutting costs, improving performance and forcing the burden of sacrifice on labour are meaningless in the face of a 40 per cent. loss of competitiveness. If the workers in, say, pulp and paper worked for nothing their product would still be uncompetitive against the dollar. Industries which were competitive three or even two years ago will go out of business. This gale of creative destruction will not just weed out the inefficient. Those who have invested and risked most are most exposed because most in debt. Others survive by trimming margins and losing money to keep markets. This process is finite.

Meanwhile the money supply cannot be controlled in the way the Thatcherites want because they will not dare to take the necessary actions: further massive spending cuts, further increases in interest rates. It requires increases of $2\frac{1}{2}$ per cent. over two years to cut money supply by 1 per cent. and the supply is well over yearly targets. Their policy has failed even in its own terms. For the real economy it has been disastrous.

Tory moderates, transmuted from Whigs to Wets, are equally stymied. Though their captain's attitude to control of M3 shows all the rationality and many of the consequences of Ahab's pursuit of the White Whale, their warnings are still muted. Yet even if they do pluck up courage to use rescue equipment it will fail without devaluation. Interest rates will fall, reluctantly and without monetarist justification. The relief will be marginal and its effects on the pound minimal when competing rates are lower. Selective aid will be offered on an increasing scale, fuel may be subsidised, the National Insurance Surcharge could be abolished; all with minimal effect on profits and investment. Even a change of Heathian dimensions is ruled out. The domestic economy cannot be expanded with an overvalued pound. Entering the EMS at a devalued rate may be a card up governmental sleeves. Yet will European competitors tolerate a substantial devaluation when they benefit so substantially from our 40 per cent. overvaluation?

The Escape from Thatcherism

If neither Thatcherism nor Wet fudging can work, the alternative must come from Labour. New policies are less important in this than an end to conditioned attitudes. We stand in awe of Finance. We have put the money economy before the real economy, attempting to show ourselves worthy of City esteem by our orthodoxy and responsibility, rather than mastering their techniques for our purposes. Our ambivalent attitudes to capitalism mean that we handle it uneasily, declining to take it into partnership as successful economies do. Our humanitarianism leads us to spend the benefits of industrial growth without achieving it. All this has to be sloughed off for Britain now faces the stark problem of industrial survival. Other nations have grown by being rigorously competitive and building up industry as the only firm basis for a strong economy. We must now follow suit, however belatedly.

The techniques are not new. Demand management of the traditional Keynesian type can pull us out of depression and put the jobless back to work. Economic growth can then allow us to change and improve to phase out the old and in the new, to invest and increase productivity in the only climate in which it will take hold, one of expansion. The declining manufacturing sector is central to growth. The faster it grows the faster the growth in G.D.P. and the greater the growth of productivity giving rise to other static and dynamic economies of scale. Exports are crucial here to sustain growth and break out of the limitations of the home market. Economies of scale apply in the internationally traded sector and investment, research and development, design, service, sales and back-up can both be improved and spread their costs over a larger and larger output.

This is the key to that virtuous circle of improving export sales leading to investment in exporting industry leading to improvements in productivity, leading to economies of scale producing increasing markets, which other countries have enjoyed. We have never done so because we have made industry the milch cow of the economy, battered it with the wild fluctuations of stop-go, crippled it with an overstrong pound. No wonder it has been unattractive to managerial talent, to investment, even to workers with skills: car workers' earnings fell by 20 per cent. relative to other workers between 1958 and 1978 while their colleagues in other countries were improving their position. Overall the earnings of skilled workers fell relative to unskilled. Since capitalism works on price signals the debilitating effect is obvious. Other countries treated industry very differently.

Demand management and industrial regeneration are the techniques. North Sea oil, by eliminating the balance-of-payments constraint and giving us the prospect of sustained growth, opens the way to use them. The problem is competitiveness. Without it industry is exposed to the gale of foreign competition, unable to reorganise or fight back. The gains from expansive demand management will wash overseas.

Restoring Competitiveness

Our disastrous competitive situation could be improved by holding our inflation well below our competitors for some years. This did not happen even in the 1920s. So only the two alternatives offer any hope. The Cambridge Economic Policy Group (C.E.P.G.) suggest tariffs, starting at 30 per cent. The less fashionable alternative is devaluation, decried by many who will say in the same breath that the pound is overvalued. Theoretical arguments between the two schools are long and complex. The prime need is for a decision since one or the other is essential. Devaluation is more effective as a basic strategy. Even the C.E.P.G. concedes that overvaluation is crippling and direct controls will be difficult if it remains. Devaluation is less likely to produce retaliation or a stultifying, introverted economy. It stimulates exports as well as hindering imports. It has worked in the past, boosting output and exports without disastrous inflation, here and for our competitors. It also allows us to isolate ourselves from world-wide deflation. There is always a rate of exchange which balances internal expansion and full employment with external equilibrium. In 1931–32 we devalued by 30 per cent., put on a tariff of 10 per cent. and negotiated tariff preferences in the Commonwealth. Unemployment fell to almost half by 1937 and in six years manufacturing output rose 64 per cent. We can do the same again by choosing a rate for sterling which suits the interests of manufacturing industry and full employment.

The measure of the value of the currency should not be prestige but our competitiveness in terms of the trade index for manufactures. Get this and our share of world trade to what both were in 1970 or the second half of 1973, and our economy is far more powerful. The initial aim can be more modest, back to 1976. This would mean getting prices down by 35 per cent., implying a devaluation of 45 per cent., bearing in mind that internal costs would rise after devaluation. Heath's devaluation increased G.D.P. by 8 per cent. in a single year. Since a much bigger squeeze has preceded ours, and manufacturing output is now 10 per cent. less than 1973 despite an investment of £26 billion since, we could aim at an increase of over 20 per cent. over a period of three years. It will be objected that devaluation increases internal inflation. Inflation is no longer the main enemy: unemployment and economic collapse are now far more dangerous. Yet a price effect more serious than this Government has already produced is unlikely.

Under-used resources on a massive scale mean expansion would bring down unit costs. Lower interest rates remove a further pressure. The Green Pound should protect us from a rise in imported food prices and if it did not there is life, and cheaper food, after the Market. Being energy rich, we set our own fuel prices. Lastly, an incomes policy, combined with price control, must mitigate inflationary pressures. A collective effort to save the economy and an incomes policy used to allocate the rewards of expansion would be more acceptable and effective than an enforced doling out of doses of deflation through wage control.

Opponents of devaluation argue that a beneficent market determines the rate. In fact Government *can* talk it down, intervene on future rates and even fix it if it wants. Yet measures designed to get the pound down are better than *dictat*. The advent of a Labour Government will have some effect. Not enough. The rapid lowering of interest rates will reverse the ratchet effect and will bring the pound down if substantial enough. Running the economy flat out also weakens the pound and should be sustained because it will change the trend of importing from manufactured goods to raw materials, machinery and semi-processed goods for completion. Then London must be made less attractive to footloose money. A tax on all money held in this country by non-residents would be one step. There should also be a withholding tax at standard rate on the interest from government stocks held by non-residents to bring them into line with other investments. The Government should begin repayment of the $20 billion of government debt held by foreigners. If the pound still obstinately refuses to come down to the preferred rate of $1.60, and *pari passu* for other currencies, the Government can announce the appropriate rate, print pounds and sell them overseas until it is reached. Money supply would expand. Yet of the three measures of money, exchange rate, interest rate and supply rate, the latter is the one best ignored.

Big bang devaluation may be inadequate. The pound not only has to be made competitive but kept so if British industry is to be encouraged to invest and plan for the long term. To encourage the investment and mark the change in national strategy, a continuing commitment to keeping industry competitive through the exchange rate, is vital. So is a continuous emphasis on exports. Our internationally traded sector has to be a focus for investment, ability and skill of which it has been starved. Exporting industries are the front line of our battle for survival. We have to use every weapon to help them to win. These weapons include tax and investment incentives for exports and long-term low-interest loans to industry to offset City caution and trigger off an investment boom. Investments grants and allowances should be increased and related to the proportion of output exported. Corporation tax could be remitted on export earnings. Tax holidays could be given to new exporting firms. Our new orientation must be written into the tax and investment system. This makes sure that we compete and grow and puts industry where it belongs, at the centre of our priorities.

For the nationalised industries a new investment programme has to reverse both the current decline and the Tory fetish of self-financing. The relegation of the National Enterprise Board must be reversed by a massive injection of capital to save the walking wounded of the Tory Paschendale and provide the risk and venture finance which our cautious capitalism has been so slow to proffer. Industry and state have to work in close and continuous co-operation. Other sectors such as the professions and the pampered personal service sector can bear greater burdens but industry is exposed to the world.

Devaluation is preferable to general import controls. Yet the plight of some essential industries is so dire that it is not enough. They need special help to break out of the downward spiral. Selective import controls will be necessary for a limited number of industries which fulfil three requirements. They must be basic to the economy in providing large numbers of jobs, having other industries dependent on them and requiring long-term, slow-yielding, investment. They must operate in fields where world trade is increasingly managed rather than free market. The state must have either control or a real and substantial influence to guarantee that the benefits of protection are seized by investment and growth. Steel, shipbuilding, coal, shipping, aerospace, perhaps cars, are the obvious candidates.

Keynesian Management Revived

The initial economic boost must come from public spending generated by borrowing and North Sea oil revenues. This can put the unemployed back to work at minimal cost. A simple calculation works thus. Average output per man is, say, £5,000 a year. A reduction in unemployment by 800,000 therefore implies extra output of £4 billion. Assuming a Keynesian multiplier (including induced investment) equal to two requires an initial expenditure injection of £2 billion. Yet the extra output generates £800 million in tax and assuming public support of, say, £2,500 per unemployed person, saves £2 billion in social security. So the initial £2 billion leads to a *smaller* P.S.B.R., cuts the overheads and generates new demand and output. At full employment the budget deficit could be zero.

The spending priorities are clear. Pensions and benefits are not immediately among them because growth and industry are the priorities. Social benefits must first be generated. Construction comes at the head of the list given its dynamic effects and its present disastrous situation. Pressing needs in industrial regeneration, housing, education, health and urban renewal co-exist with massive unemployment of workers and resources.

The Uses of Money

To back competitiveness Labour needs a financial policy, an anti-monetarism. Like manure, money has to be well and cheaply spread. So the Government's hand must be strengthened in money matters to make *it* the master, not the markets, and to give it effective power over interest rates. Keynes advocated the socialisation of investment. Half a century later we still have not achieved it.

Nationalisation of the Bank of England is a farce if the Bank can impose the City's views on the Government. Control over the banking system must be restored. A politician in charge of the Bank would see that it follows Cabinet policy, its officials should be interchangeable with Whitehall, and those controls which were swept away by Competition and Credit Control in 1971 should be brought back, extended and supplemented by measures controlling hire-purchase and credit cards, imposing differential reserve requirements and taxing less essential lending. We can exercise selective control of credit.

The aim is to channel credit and reduce interest rates, a return to the days of cheap money with an M.L.R. of 6 per cent. Interest rates should be a means of building the economy and stimulating investment, not controlling the money supply. If the City refuses to buy government stock at appropriate rates its bluff can be called by printing money. Government is entitled to refuse to finance the whole of its borrowing requirement. The printing press should be an instrument of policy. Resources of men, plant, machinery, are now seriously under-employed, perhaps to the extent of a quarter of overall capacity. Increases in money supply will make resources productive or be saved, in which case the supply of money increases relative to demand and interest rates will fall. Such a stimulus can hardly be inflationary if money use and economic activity are brought into balance and proper controls are used to avoid the side effects of growth becoming, as they did under Heath, a splurge of property speculation, funny-money manipulation, asset stripping and fringe-bank bonanza.

Conclusion: Back to Full Employment

A depressing air of unreality suffuses Britain's economic debate. The public is relapsing into despair. Thatcherism is generating its own mirror images and making more conceivable that capitalist collapse in which they would thrive. All this is happening as North Sea oil gives Britain her first chance of growing by removing that balance-of-payments constraint which has strangled every previous effort. The Conservative Party is going too far down a dead-end street, so the alternative can now only come from Labour. Sticking to tired old deflationary orthodoxies will not provide it. Nor will a return to socialist basics which change structures but leave economic problems unresolved. Britain's problems, hence Labour's, centre on competitiveness. Growth and clear-headed economics are the guides to solving both. Painful as our present learning process may be, it gives us the chance to consign the whole deflationary syndrome to the dustbin of history before it does the same for Britain. To do so we must apply ourselves to the long-overdue task of working out our alternative and proclaiming it to a nation losing hope.

Britain is steadily becoming Europe's scrounger, a mean, divided, creaking society in which blame is the general chorus and the political struggle is worse than that zero-sum game which dominates the politics of nil growth. With actual decline the struggle becomes sub-zero sub-sum, super-nasty. With a viable alternative to Thatcherism Britain can reverse decline and restore full employment and economic growth. No party dedicated to the interests of the multitude who labour can do more. Crosland made clear the extent to which socialism depends on growth. It is up to us, a quarter of a century later, to show how it can be achieved in a far harsher, colder world than he ever envisaged.

THE NORTH EAST:
BACK TO THE 1930s?

BEN PIMLOTT

UNEMPLOYMENT is higher in the Northern Region than in any other part of Great Britain.[1] This maintains a long tradition. In the North East unemployment was massive between the wars, and markedly above average after 1945. As a result a knowledge if not an expectation of life on the dole is part of the working-class heritage. In areas like the West Midlands, where the job shortage is new, unemployment is seen as a bewildering aberration. In Newcastle and Middlesbrough, by contrast, there is a battening down of hatches with a weary sense of the return of a familiar adversary.

" The spectre of a return to the thirties has become a frightening reality ", wrote the authors of a study of unemployment in Newcastle two years ago.[2] Today, the pre-war slump is in everybody's mind. Recalling the past, people view the future with an understandable foreboding. The prognosis for the region is certainly bad. However, despite surface similarities, a simple identification of this depression with the one of 50 years ago is misleading.

Back to the 1930s?

The North East is still an area of old industries in decline. Shipbuilding, engineering, metal manufacture, whose contraction caused chronic unemployment before the war, have all been making workers redundant in the present slump. However, the proportion of the workforce in these industries had already shrunk dramatically before the 1970s, as part of a major revolution in the economy of the region. The biggest changes in the post-war period were a sharp decline in coal-mining, a fast growth of light industry, and a rapid

* The author is Visiting Research Associate in the Department of International History, London School of Economics. He is the author of *Labour and the Left in the 1930s* (Cambridge University Press, 1977). He thanks Keith Hodgson, Andrew Gillespie, Joe Mills, John March, Nick Anderson, Gary Craig, Chris Edwards, Martin Upham and John Griffiths, among others, for help in preparing this article. The views expressed are, however, entirely his own.

[1] 11·7 per cent. (excluding school-leavers) on September 11, 1980. The Northern Region (as defined by the Department of Employment) is composed of 22 Travel-to-Work Areas bounded by Berwick (in the North), Teesside (in the South East) and Whitehaven (in the West). When I refer to the " North East " I mean the 14—largely industrial—Areas in the East of this region, where seven-eighths of the population lives, and where unemployment is generally higher than in the other more sparsely inhabited Areas.

[2] Benwell Community Project, *Permanent Unemployment* (1978).

increase in employment in the public services sector. Pit closures in the 1930s produced unemployment figures of 80 per cent. or more in many Durham villages. By the 1970s, few communities remained that were solely or even largely dependent on coal. Transport, communications, metal manufacture, shipbuilding, distributive trades, agriculture and fishing all shed workers in the decade 1965–75. Yet the combined total of jobs lost in all these industries was less than the number in the Northern Region who left mining and quarrying in the same period: 69,000 in all. Some ex-miners left the area, and others retired early. But many remained, making up a large pool of de-skilled surplus labour. Since the late 1930s, the prospect of employing cheap labour had attracted light industry to the region, and it was the aim of successive post-war regional policies to encourage this trend. The 1960s saw the final phase, with the introduction of plastics and rubber-based production, and the expansion of the hosiery and knitted goods industries and other types of light manufacture.

How successful were attempts by post-war governments to steer the growth generated by firms in the prosperous Midlands and South to the North East? Many companies came, or established new branches. For a long time, however, the disparity between local and national unemployment rates remained remarkably stable. From the late 1960s the gap began gradually to narrow, suggesting that the problem of a North Eastern regional pocket of unemployment was at last being brought under control. The narrowing was especially marked during the sharp 1975–76 recession, in which the North East seemed to be less affected than the rest of the country. Thus, by the beginning of 1976, the difference between regional and national unemployment had become smaller than at any other time in the decade.[3] But this relative improvement was short-lived. During the last four years, unemployment in the North East has grown faster than the national average, restoring the old differential. Was the relative improvement, or the subsequent deterioration, part of a long-term trend? It is likely that the factors which caused things to get better up to 1976 had little to do with the basic industrial health of the region. Thus increases in public sector services employment (accelerated by local government and health service reorganisation) were important, and so was a growth in local spending power caused by a sharp increase in earnings among manual

[3] A. Gillespie and D. Owen, " The Relationship between National and Local Unemployment Rates: A Case Study of the Northern Region 1971–80 " (SSRC Paper, 1980).

groups over-represented in the region. After 1976 such accidental advantages ceased to apply.

Moreover, in the new economic storm the light industry which had been attracted to the region in the 1960s and earlier—whether by relative factor costs or government incentives—was seriously affected as well. Many of the new factories were owned, or had been acquired, by large firms based outside the region, or by multi-national companies. " Uncle Sam has a big stake in the North East ", a local paper commented cheerfully when President Carter visited Newcastle in 1977: " 30,000 Geordies are on his payroll ".[4] It was calculated in the same year that 76 companies in the region were American-owned, a symptom of a growing concentration of control of jobs among a decreasing number of large firms or consortia: Northern Engineering Industries, Dunlop, Ever Ready, Courtaulds, GEC, Thorn prominent among them. Involvement by large concerns, especially those with major interests abroad, now began to reveal its less attractive side. A tendency to switch investments to other low-wage areas overseas became apparent; so did a pattern in which big firms having bought up little firms used their new North Eastern subsidiaries as marketing outlets rather than for production, or shut them down altogether. One calculation suggests that about two-thirds of closures involving more than 30 redundancies in 1979 in Tyne and Wear were of factories acquired, through purchase or merger, by a larger concern. Similarly, in the first seven months of 1980, over half the private employers laying off more than 30 workers were linked to " multi-nationals ", broadly defined.

Thus the decline of the new manufacturing sector has compounded the effects of the contraction of traditional industries, producing a sharply worsening position over the last four years in the South Tyneside, Wearside, Teesside and Hartlepool Areas in particular. There have been local crises. In Hartlepool, the high rate (15·9 per cent.) is because of steel closures and severe cutbacks. On Teesside (13·7 per cent.), a large number of redundancies in construction followed the completion of the huge blastfurnace at Redcar. In addition, capital-intensive investment by ICI has resulted in a thinning of the workforce—with an expectation of a further 25 per cent. reduction over the next five years. The most devastating blow of all struck the steel town of Consett in September, when the decision by BSC to cease production created 3,700 redundancies and raised the unemployment level overnight to an estimated 40 per cent.

4 Benwell and North Tyneside C.D.P., *Multinationals in Tyne and Wear* (1979).

More than any other event, the extinguishing of the furnaces in Consett brought back memories of the 1930s and of the closure of Palmer's Shipyard in 1933, which gave Jarrow a place in history as " The Town that was Murdered " with two-thirds of its workers on the dole. There are fears that Consett is just the beginning. It is arguable, however, that if unemployment continues to grow it will tend to do so, not in concentrated lumps, but evenly across the region. Apart from Consett, where the long-term rate is not yet known, no Area is more than 4.2 per cent. above the level for the region as a whole. This is partly because there are few one-industry towns. It is also because of the greater diversity of work even where industry is concentrated. Not only are there new, small factories producing a wide range of goods scattered through much of the region, there has also been a massive growth in public sector services employment (health, education, local and national government). For a generation, the expansion of this kind of work from a low base has masked the erosion of jobs elsewhere. Today, one worker in five is employed by a local or national authority—providing an important cushion against cyclical fluctuations. Even in Consett, more people worked for schools, hospitals or local government than for British Steel.

Women Workers in the North East

Public sector services are, of course, not invulnerable. Cash limits imposed by central government are likely to take their toll. So is modern technology. Communications has already been affected. Many white-collar jobs are now under threat. The huge DHSS " clerical factory " at Longbenton in Newcastle is expected to shed a large part of its 12,000—mainly female—workforce as a result of computerisation. In general, however, public sector services employment provides a degree of security which the private sector can no longer offer. This is particularly true for women workers. The official figure for female unemployment in the Northern Region (9.7 per cent.) is much more unreliable than the male statistic (13.0 per cent.) because women often fail to register, or remove themselves from the job market. Nevertheless, the gap between regional and national levels of unemployment is greater for women than for men, suggesting that women are faring worse in comparison to men in the North East than elsewhere. This is in itself a product of the changed economic structure of the region. The North East has been traditionally an area of low female activity. In the 1930s, when there was little work for men, paid employment for women outside the home barely existed. After the war, female activity rapidly increased and by the 1970s it had begun to approach the rate for the nation as a whole. In 1971, 40 per cent. of women over 15 in the Northern Region were economically active, a rise of 8·7 per cent. over the decade, compared with an increase of only 5·3 per cent. nationally.[5]

The accusation is sometimes made that female employment has put men on the dole, and it is certainly true that if all unemployed men took over jobs done by women, there would still be more female employment than existed in the 1930s. However, such a calculation ignores the nature of the jobs available for women: usually unskilled, short-term and part-time, generally low paid, almost always poorly unionised, and with a high turnover. These features, which made female labour attractive to the new manufacturers of the 1960s, also place women on the vulnerable margin of employability in time of recession. Indeed, the " feminisation " of the workforce—the growing proportion of the labour market that is composed of women—is one sign of the declining demand for skills in an area where the percentage of skilled workers has been traditionally high. One effect of unemployment has been to de-skill the skilled, and repeated studies have shown how workers have been forced to seek jobs which do not make use of their qualifications or experience, gradually swelling the huge army of the unskilled, among whom competition for work is most fierce, and for whom jobs are worst paid and most casual. In some occupations, job loss almost inevitably means a change of trade, or the acceptance of less-skilled work. Thus, in March 1980, there were more than 90 unemployed platers and welders for each notified vacancy in the region.[6]

The General Labourer

The ratio of men seeking work within the category officially described as " general labourers " is so bad that a prolonged period of unemployment is almost certain for anybody made redundant who falls within it. Table 1 (which compares the Northern Region with the South East) shows how false is the belief that unemployment is much the same problem everywhere, or that the variations around the country are less important than the common features.

Of course, these figures give no indication of the actual competition for jobs in each region or category. As many as two-thirds of all

[5] M. J. Moseley and Jane Darby, " The Importance of F.A.R.", *Regional Studies* (1978).
[6] *Regional Employment Market Intelligence Trends* (M.S.C. Northern Region) (Spring 1980).

TABLE 1

Ratios of Unemployed to Notified Vacancies (excluding school-leavers)
August 1980

	South East Region	Northern Region
Managerial and Professional	3·8	6·0
Clerical	3·8	14·2
Other non-manual	2·0	10·9
Craft, foremen, etc.	2·5	12·9
Semi-skilled	2·8	10·2
General labourers	40·8	172·5
All	3·9	17·6

vacancies are never notified, and this proportion varies between groups. Also, far more workers are listed in the bottom category than properly belong in it. What is interesting is the contrast between the two regions. Even allowing for scaling down and a wide margin of error, the table suggests that there are more than four times as many unemployed for each vacancy in the Northern Region as in the South East. In both regions, there is the same concentration at the bottom. In the Northern Region, however, there are fiercely unfavourable ratios in all categories except the highest, whereas in the South East, skilled and clerical workers are relatively immune. The incomprehension of the politically influential Southern professional—who may still find it hard to get a good secretary—is partly explained by these figures.

The table also reveals, once again, the danger of a simple analogy with the last great slump. A feature of the 1930s was a steady migration of younger men from Tyneside and the Durham coalfields to the South and Midlands. In 1934, when unemployment was 67·8 per cent. in Jarrow, it was only 3·9 per cent. in St. Albans and 5·1 per cent. in Oxford. Today, however, there are no boom towns to take on the surplus labour of other regions. Making workers go to the work is no good if there is no work to be had. For the worst affected category—the unskilled—the South East offers little hope. One effect of unemployment has been not to increase movement away from the North East, but to reduce it.

The Social Impact

It is commonly believed among people whose lives are insulated from the realities of unemployment that joblessness is a problem only for those without work. This is quite untrue. Anxiety and frustration

56

arising from insecurity and from an inability to change jobs affect a high proportion of those in work, and fear of redundancy determines the mood of the whole region to an extent that outsiders find hard to understand. As unemployment rises, those with jobs start looking over their shoulders. Older people are the most frightened, but younger people are affected too. "The over 45s tend to hang on to their jobs like grim death—whatever the working conditions and pay", comments one trade unionist. "The under 30s have increasingly come to expect their work to be of limited duration."

Those with work and those without it have more in common than is at first apparent. As the jobless total rises, so does the likelihood of a period of unemployment for those currently holding jobs. The unemployment statistic is like a transit camp, through which many more people pass than are at any one time in it—and which people will visit more frequently and occupy longer the more crowded it gets. Among the unskilled, frequent spells of unemployment have long been a normal experience in the North East. A survey of economically active men in an area of North Shields where male unemployment was currently 16 per cent. showed that almost half were either unemployed at the time of interview or had been in the recent past.[7] In periods of relatively full employment, the decision to give up work for a short period may be a rational option. This choice ceases to be available for most people when jobs are scarce. As unemployment rises, so does the "expectation of worklessness". The North East not only has more people on the dole than elsewhere but unemployment tends to last much longer. In April 1980, 48 per cent. of the unemployed in the Northern Region have been out of work for more than six months, and 17 per cent. for more than two years, compared with 37 per cent. and 11 per cent. in the South East. Given the disparity in unemployment rates between the two regions, this means that almost three times as high a proportion of the total workforce had been unemployed for more than six months in the Northern Region (5·6 per cent.) as in the South East (2·0 per cent.). Since long-term unemployment always goes on rising after the turning-point of aggregate unemployment, this feature is bound to get worse.

For many workers the problem does not end when a job is eventually found. A period of unemployment often precipitates a downward spiral. Those affected often have to accept worse-paid and

[7] North Tyneside C.D.P., *In and Out of Work* (1978). The survey was carried out in 1976.

less-secure work than they had before, and are the most likely to be dropped in the next economic contraction. The North Shields study showed that two-thirds of the men currently unemployed had been in and out of work for years. A third had been among the low paid (as defined by the Low Pay Unit) when last in work, but their last job often did not reflect their highest skill in recent years.[8] Experience in the North East suggests that in a deepening recession the condition of being unemployed is like a disease, hard to shake off, and most likely to be contracted by the economically weak and marginal: the over-45s, school-leavers, the unskilled, the disabled.

Real poverty rapidly affected those put out of work and unable to find a new job. Fewer than half of the unemployed among the North Shields sample were receiving unemployment benefit, the rest having exhausted their entitlement. Seven out of 10 were on supplementary benefit. The study did not lend support to the view that many people prefer unemployment because the financial advantages of working are so slight. Only a quarter of the unemployed men were within 20 per cent. of their income from work when they were employed, without taking account of the means-tested benefits many could have claimed if they had been working. One effect of the " poverty trap ", however, was that wives often stopped work when their husbands became unemployed or when they started to collect supplementary benefit.[9]

Sometimes the pill of redundancy is sweetened with redundancy pay. Management and unions have both found that workers are often more than willing to take a large lump sum as the price for their job. The advantage even of a substantial redundancy payment, however, is often far less than its cash value suggests. The means testing of supplementary benefit cuts the real value sharply after the first few months. Moreover, redundancy pay can make a period of unemployment more likely. A study of workers made redundant after the closure of Adamsez Ltd., a sanitary-ware factory in Scotswood, Newcastle, suggested that fear of losing redundancy money reduced the incentive to look for alternative work in advance of the shutdown.[10]

Not all unemployment is recurrent, and most is not permanent. A year after the Tress Engineering Company in Newcastle closed in June 1978 only a third of the 350 workers made redundant were still

8 Ibid.
9 Ibid.
10 Benwell Community Project, Adamsez: The Story of a Factory Closure (1980), p. 53.

without jobs.[11] Among former workers at Adamsez, 88 per cent. had found work within two years, though many had taken jobs they liked less. Significantly, a high proportion had got work through family connections rather than through orthodox channels. Elsewhere, especially in smaller communities, family links are even more important, as are social contacts which cost money to maintain. The fishing and holiday town of Whitby [12] has a level of unemployment which has long been among the highest in the country (and will shortly be increased as a result of 650 redundancies at the nearby potash mine at Boulby). This is how a local postal worker describes the business of seeking work:

" There are tried and tested strategies available to our people when they lose their jobs. Some of our activities have always been on the fringe of the black economy or worse. Coastal fishing and taking fishing parties have always operated on a cash in hand basis, as has poaching. To make use of the opportunities here, you must belong to the appropriate family network or be acceptable to it. The traditional values of thrift and abstemiousness can actually be counter-productive if you lose your job. Most job information is available in pubs and this is particularly true of ' fringe ' opportunities. I found when I was out of work that the place that had most rumours and chances was the Working Men's Club. This is at its most active between 2.30 and 4.0 p.m. when a fair bit of drinking is done and also some pretty heavy gambling. To be part of this you need some ready cash."

As unemployment grows, so the need to make use of such techniques increases, and the possibility of finding work without the right connections gets less. " Employment is like a tide ", a government official has written: " When full, it draws in almost all adult men and a high proportion of adult women. As it recedes, those least attractive to employers tend to get stranded first. If a recession deepens, others, many of whom will never have been unemployed before, become stranded also." [13] The last 10 years have seen a steady extension of the social territory in which unemployment is an expected state.

The young form the largest new group of those least attractive to employers. Between January 1971 and January 1978 unemployment among people under 20 rose in the Northern Region from 14 per cent. to 20 per cent., declining slightly in the following year under the impact of the Youth Opportunities Programme, before rising

[11] City of Newcastle upon Tyne Policy Service Department, *Redundancy in Newcastle upon Tyne: a case study* (1980).

[12] Whitby is just outside the Northern Region as defined by the Department of Employment, but has many links with County Cleveland and Teesside.

[13] R. Harrison, " The Demoralising Effects of Long-term Unemployment ", *Employment Gazette* (April 1976).

again in 1979–80. The problem is exacerbated by the low proportion of children in the North East who stay at school beyond the age of 16. In towns like North Shields, Sunderland, Hartlepool and Consett, and also in the big urban centres of Tyneside and Teesside, most school-leavers expect to go on to the dole. Older children in Newcastle schools are taught how to sign on for social security, and everywhere there is a coffee-bar society of unemployed teenagers. Again, the distinction between the employed and unemployed is ill-defined, as much of the work available to the young is temporary, and so to be " between jobs " is part of a normal pattern.

Thus unemployment in the North East is having insidious long-term effects, which go beyond the breakdowns, suicide and divorce which highlight the tragedy in individual cases, or the poverty that affects those who are out of work for any length of time. The North Eastern experience shows how false is the comfortable belief that while inflation hurts everybody, unemployment only affects the unfortunate minority who make up the statistics.

The Politics of Unemployment

Unemployment causes bitterness and fear. But it would be wrong to assume from this that there will be a strong political or industrial backlash. On the contrary, few regions are likely to cause politicians less anxiety than the North East, for several reasons.

Most of the North East is safe for Labour. Of 29 constituencies, 25 are Labour-held, one is Liberal and only three are Conservative. Labour has hopes of winning all three Tory seats, and in a land-slide victory might conceivably do so—but only one, Newcastle North, is really marginal.[14] A big swing to the Right could give the Tories Darlington, and the solitary Liberal at Berwick is always vulnerable in a traditionally Conservative seat. Nothing else is likely to change hands without an electoral revolution. The political parties realise this, and during election campaigns it is extremely hard to get leading politicians to spend time in an area where so little is at stake.

Conservative hopes of making even minor inroads into this un-promising territory must be dampened by evidence of a continuing pro-Labour drift in voting behaviour. This has accelerated over the last generation, though it was perceptible by 1964.[15] It probably has

14 The boundaries of Newcastle North are likely to be radically changed before the next election.
15 D. E. Butler and D. Stokes, *Political Change in Britain* (1969), p. 136.

little directly to do with unemployment. One of the biggest relative improvements in Labour's position occurred at the last election, when most North Eastern seats under-swung to the Right, and one, Teesside Thornaby, actually swung the other way. Yet this was after a period of Labour Government during which unemployment had grown even faster in the North East than elsewhere—widening the gap between nation and region which had narrowed under Mr. Heath. Arguably, the " de-skilling " effect of recession and unemployment keeps a larger proportion of the electorate in the poorer manual groups where Labour voting is most common. Apart from this gradual strengthening of Labour's base, there is nothing in the voting record of the region to make any party hopeful or alarmed. The North East has a much stronger sense of regional identity than most other industrial areas in England. But unlike Scotland, Wales or Northern Ireland there is no third force or separatist movement that needs to be assuaged.

Thus, in Westminster and electoral terms, the North East is a part of the country which the Conservatives can afford to ignore. Of the three Tory M.P.s in the region, only one, Geoffrey Rippon, carries any weight among his colleagues, and none have influence in the Government. On the Labour side, the North Eastern M.P.s can sometimes have more power. Regional unemployment and resentment at the financial terms of the Scottish settlement were major factors in the successful opposition of a number of North Eastern M.P.s to the proposed Scottish Assembly in 1979. In situations other than the hung Parliament of 1974–79, the Northern Group of Labour M.P.s is an important political phalanx within the PLP: a strong pressure for regional aid and (when Labour is in office) a powerful lobby for government contracts. But with Labour in Opposition, no region has less parliamentary bargaining power.

According to one view, the deepening depression will force the working class to make its voice heard in radical, even non-constitutional ways. There is no evidence to support this in the North East. Trade unions and the Labour Party in the region have been traditionally " moderate ", and M.P.s include several prominent members of the Manifesto Group: William Rodgers, Ian Wrigglesworth, John Horam, Giles Radice, Mike Thomas. " Very recently ", comments one, " the young unemployed have strengthened the Militant Left and enabled their case to get a better hearing." Yet no M.P. has had any serious trouble from his GMC on political grounds. Despite a conviction in the media that CLP activists are usually extremists, many constituency parties do not really divide along a Left-Right axis at all. The far Left (Trotskyist or Communist) is weaker in the North East than elsewhere, and weaker now than it was even 10 years ago, when memories of the 1930s were fresher.

There is no sign of an industrial reaction to unemployment either. "Unfortunately, unemployment has not stimulated any shop floor activity", observes the regional organiser of one of the largest unions. "Actually, quite the reverse. What we find is that when companies declare redundancies and we encourage some resistance then we find that members are prepared to accept redundancy pay and make a quick exit." When the T. & G.W.U. in Newcastle offered to make a stand over the Consett closure, by bringing transport in the region to a halt and closing the Tyne Docks, the plan was dropped because the response from the steelworkers was lukewarm. Similarly, the workforce at NEI Reyrolle in Newcastle rejected a recommendation from shop stewards to resist 800 redundancies.

So far from causing resistance to employers, unemployment has had the effect of reducing wage demands and discouraging industrial action. Willingness to compromise at levels lower than the inflation rate has become the pattern. It was symptomatic that a seven-week official strike at the Ronson plant at Cramlington in Co. Durham in the summer of 1980 ended when the workers went back to work on the employers' terms. As one trade unionist put it: "The whole gloomy story is getting through to the workers". For the first time since the war, the fear of forcing or providing an excuse for closures has begun seriously to inhibit wage bargaining.

Unions themselves have been hard hit by redundancies, which cut their membership and their income. Very few workers remain union members, even at a much reduced rate, when they go on the dole. The T. & G.W.U. has lost 7,000 members and £180,000 in dues because of lay-offs in the Northern Region over the 12 months to October 1980. Others have suffered similar losses, and there is concern lest falling membership should cause friction between unions in the future because of competition in recruitment.

There is little sign of organisation or militancy among the unemployed themselves—no recrudescence of Wal Hannington's pre-war National Unemployed Workers' Movement, the Communist-led association which campaigned against the Means Test and helped to bring about the Jarrow March. In April 1979 a group of young trade unionists in Newcastle set up an Unemployed Workers' Union. With the aid of grants from trade unions and the Priority Area Team (funded by the local authority and the Department of the

Environment), this now has an enthusiastic paid organiser, a crumbling office on the quayside, and 52 paid-up members. Similar unions for the unemployed have been set up in Durham, Darlington, Spennymoor and Middlesbrough, and there is an unemployed centre in Stockton. The Newcastle union sees itself as an information centre and as a pressure group—giving advice to those on the dole, and making their case heard in the City. A recent minor victory was to persuade local cinemas to offer one free afternoon to unemployed teenagers. It was pointed out that the normal cost of a ticket is a fifth of a 16-year-old's weekly social security.

Thus unemployment is having a colossal economic, social and psychological impact on the whole of the North East, and in time this will take a political form. But it is wishful thinking to imagine that there will be repercussions for any government that neglects the region, or that North Easterners will somehow force a change for the better. This did not happen before the war, and it is even less likely to happen now. Compared with 50 years ago unemployment in the North East is less concentrated, less dramatic and as yet much less severe, and the unemployed are usually better off. The 1980s will not be like the 1930s, when most people in the North East were almost unimaginably poor, and some were close to starvation. The tragedy of the next decade may well be, instead, that a chronically high and growing rate of unemployment with all its evil consequences gradually becomes something which everybody takes for granted.

DE-INDUSTRIALISATION AND UNEMPLOYMENT IN THE WEST MIDLANDS

STAN TAYLOR

THE West Midland standard region comprises the counties of Salop, Staffordshire, Hereford and Worcester and Warwickshire along with the conurbation belt stretching from Coventry to Birmingham and through to Dudley, Sandwell, Walsall and Wolverhampton. The region experienced high levels of employment throughout most of the period 1945–75; unemployment rates were almost always below the national average, although the disparity was more marked prior to 1964 than afterwards. In 1975–76 the regional unemployment rate climbed above the national mean, and fluctuated within a decimal point of the overall figure during the remainder of the 1970s. In 1980, the rate rose significantly above the average, increasing from 5·7 per cent. in January to 9·4 per cent. in September compared to the national increase from 5·9 to 8·4 per cent. The percentage rise in the West Midlands was greater than that in any other part of the United Kingdom, and the region fell in 1980 from fifth place in the regional employment rankings to sixth, its lowest position in the post-war period. If the various economic forecasters are to be believed, this relative decline will continue. The Cambridge Economic Policy Review Group [1] has predicted that by 1983 unemployment in the West Midlands will reach 13·7 per cent., higher than in any other part of Britain except Northern Ireland and Wales; the Manpower Research Group at the University of Warwick [2] has projected that one in five males will be out of work by the mid-1980s. Given that the regional average combines high rates of unemployment in the conurbation belt and lower ones in most of the non-metropolitan county areas, it seems likely that the proportion out of work in Coventry, Birmingham and the Black Country towns will rise even above these levels and, among men at least, be comparable to those experienced during the interwar depression. The major difference will be that whereas in the 1930s unemploy-

* The author lectures in Politics, University of Warwick.
[1] *Cambridge Economic Policy Review* (Vol. 6, No. 2, July 1980).
[2] G. T. Keogh and P. Elias, "Regional Employment Prospects", in R. Lindley (ed.), *Economic Change and Economic Policy* (Macmillan, 1980).

ment in the northern and Scottish conurbations was considerably higher than in the West Midlands, by the mid-1980s only the Welsh valleys and Belfast will have more unemployment than the West Midlands. Only a few years ago it was almost inconceivable that, for example, Coventry could replace Tyneside as the unemployment black spot of England; now it is probable. How has this change come about?

The Long-Term Background to Unemployment

The West Midlands has been immunised from major structural change in the economy during the past by the skills of its workers. The industrial prosperity of the region was founded upon its basic industries, including coal and steel, and upon metal-working. When the basic industries began to decline, their place was taken by engineering industries, including the bicycle, car and aircraft industries, which could utilise the skills of the metal workers. The suppliers of these industries were attracted to the West Midlands, and these in turn drew other firms until the region became the main centre for manufacturing industry in Britain. In the interwar years unemployment levels were lower than those in most parts of Britain, and recovery from depression was more rapid. Rearmament in the late 1930s acted as a further boost to the vehicle and aircraft industries and their suppliers, so that the region became one of net immigration as workers came from outside to gain employment. In the immediate post-war period the factories were re-equipped to produce vehicles and aircraft for European export markets starved by the wartime destruction of productive capacity. The progressive loss of these markets, which began in the mid-1950s as the rest of Europe recovered, was more than compensated for by the growth of a home market for private cars following the removal of petrol rationing in 1953 and the easing of restrictions upon credit for car purchase in 1954. The boom led to shortages of labour; this, coupled with strong union organisation and managements prepared to buy out trouble at almost any price to keep the lines rolling, led to high incomes. By the early 1960s the West Midlands was established as a high-employment high-wage sub-economy. The earnings and spending power of its workers became legendary, and there was much sociological speculation as to whether affluence and consumption fever had eroded the basis of working-class solidarity and led to the creation of a new blue-collar middle class with manual jobs but middle-class incomes, lifestyles and class self-identifications. While doubt has been cast upon the embourgeoisement of the car worker, this does not alter the picture of unprecedented working-class affluence; by 1964, the earnings of male manual workers in the West Midlands were higher than in any other part of Britain, more than 17 per cent. above the national average. As in the 1930s this industrial Eldorado attracted workers from other parts of Britain and Eire: additionally many came from the New Commonwealth. Nearly all of these found jobs. Unemployment only occurred when there was a " hiccup " in the demand for cars or when workers were in transition from one highly paid job to another even more highly paid.

The early 1960s proved to be the zenith of the region's prosperity. By 1966, nearly one-half of the workforce was employed in the manufacturing sector of the economy, more than in any other region of the country. As in other advanced economies, this sector has declined markedly relative to the service sector as economic development has proceeded. Over the country as a whole between 1965 and 1976, employment in manufacturing declined by 15 per cent. This decline had more impact in the West Midlands than elsewhere because of the importance of manufacturing in the region; but additionally trends of decline within manufacturing industry made the position relatively worse. The highest rates of decline were in metals, metal goods, instrument engineering and vehicles, precisely those industries which were dominant in the West Midlands. From the 1960s onwards the trials and tribulations of the motor industry, the main single source of employment, are too well-known to bear repetition. It is sufficient to note that, by the mid-1970s, the major motor firms in the region and some of their suppliers were reliant upon public funds for their continued operation.

Over the country as a whole, growth within the service sector and in a few manufacturing industries offset the general decline in manufacturing to the extent that in 1976 there was only one in 40 fewer jobs than in 1965. In the West Midlands, there was less compensating growth in employment, and by 1976 the region had lost one-twentieth of the jobs it had had in 1965. The cause of this lies in considerable measure in the reluctance of successive governments to concede that the presence of skilled workers in the region was insufficient to protect it from de-industrialisation and that it required assistance beyond whatever proportion of the funds given to the motor industry found their way to the region. Between 1972 and mid-1979, governments paid out nearly £2,000 million in regional development aid. Only £2·4 million of this (0·1 per cent.) went to the West Midlands. Under the last Labour Government's Job Creation Programmes, 140,000 jobs were created nationally. The resource input in the West Midlands was such that only 7,500 jobs, 5·0 per cent. of the total, were created in the region. Governments did not direct their own office jobs towards the region. While employment in public administration increased nationally by 18 per cent. 1965–76, that in the West Midlands rose by only 9 per cent., less than in any other region bar Wales, and more than 20 per cent. less than the East Midlands, the North West, the North, Scotland and Northern Ireland.

Unemployment in 1980

Given the reliance of the West Midlands upon manufacturing industry, its parlous state at the end of the 1970s, and the dependence of a number of firms upon state funding, it was not surprising that the policies of the Conservative Government elected in 1979 turned gentle decline into quickening collapse. High interest rates and a strong pound disproportionately penalised the manufacturing sector upon which the region depended; pre-existing weakness meant that firms closed rather than cut back as in other regions of the country. The selling of National Enterprise Board holdings like Alfred Herberts in Coventry cost jobs because the private firms which bought them were unwilling to sustain the labour force at existing levels. The attachment of conditions for State aid to BL resulted in redundancies through rationalisation (*i.e.* plant closures) or modernisation (the introduction of new machines to replace workers). The closure of major plants had a " ripple " effect through the regional economy as primary and secondary suppliers were forced to dismiss workers.

Redundancies were one source of rapidly increasing unemployment in the West Midlands, another was a bulge in the size of the population seeking their first job. In the 1950s and the 1960s, the affluence and high employment of the region attracted many immigrants from both inside and outside Britain. These mobile workers were, in the main, in their 20s and early 30s when they moved, and by the mid-1960s the West Midlands had a disproportionate number of people within this age-range compared to other regions. These people settled in the area, married and had children. The consequence some 16 years later was that an above-average proportion of the population were young and looking for work. This fact increased the rate of unemployment in the West Midlands; but, in addition, unemployment among the young was higher than among comparable groups in other regions. This in part reflected rapid de-industrialisation making fewer jobs available, and in part another feature of the West Midlands population, the relatively high proportion of the young who were members of ethnic minority groups. The children of the New Commonwealth immigrants of the 1960s who settled more in the West Midlands than in many other regions faced not only the disadvantage of being young but also discrimination because of their colour. The latter problem was not of course confined to the young from the ethnic minorities, and older workers suffered more from high unemployment rates than non-minority workers. A study of unemployment in Birmingham in 1977–78 [3] found that older ethnic minority workers were twice as likely as others to be unemployed, and it seems likely that their relative position would have worsened as recession deepened in 1980. Thus the disproportionate presence of ethnic minority workers among the West Midlands population was a factor in explaining a more rapid growth of unemployment in 1980 than in other regions.

The Impact of Unemployment

The most obvious place to see how the extremes of life in the West Midlands affected a community was Coventry, once the most affluent of the West Midlands cities, now likely to become among the most deprived. The city suffered less from unemployment in the 1930s than either the West Midlands region or the nation as a whole. When J. B. Priestley visited it in 1933 [4] he found it well on its way to recovery and commented that Coventry " seemed to have acquired the trick of keeping up with the times, a trick that many of our industrial cities find hard to learn "; it " made bicycles when everyone was cycling, cars when everyone wanted a motor, and now it is also busy with aeroplanes, wireless sets and various electrical contrivances ". These industries boomed during the war and in the post-war period Coventry became the unofficial capital of the motor industry and an important location of the aircraft industry. By 1961, these growth industries accounted for one-half of male employment in the city. The Coventry engineering workers were the best-paid in the country, with wages between one-third and one-fifth higher than comparable workers elsewhere. The affluence of the workers was apparent to Graham Turner when he met with some while interviewing for his book *The Car Makers* (Pelican, 1962). The Coventry workers owned their own homes, had cars, spent often and rapidly,

---

[3] A. Barber, "Ethnic Origin and the Labour Force", *Employment Gazette* (August 1980).

[4] J. B. Priestley, *English Journey* (Pelican, 1977).

and regarded the professional classes with "pity, not awe" and white-collar workers with "lofty disdain". Their prosperity seemed secure and unemployment in Coventry only rose above the national average in two of the years between 1945 and 1970 (in 1956 and 1957). The departure of part of the aircraft industry and the end of expansion of the car industry in the late 1960s had a minor impact upon the city, but in 1969 it was still buoyant with wages one-third above the average and low unemployment.

The first intimations of difficulty came in the 1971–72 recession, when unemployment did increase beyond the national level, and the Rolls Royce engine plant was taken into public ownership. But Coventry, it was assumed, would adapt as it always had done. As one academic study in 1972[5] concluded "generally the prospects are very bright. That industry which Coventry does have is for the greater part thriving, while at the same time it has a young and highly skilled workforce." Optimism was scarcely dented by the near-collapse of the car industry in the mid-1970s. In 1975 Coventry's Chrysler plants were only saved from closure by a government loan of £162 million, British Leyland with five major plants in the city was nationalised, and the Coventry toolmaking firm Alfred Herbert was taken under the wing of the National Enterprise Board. This effectively meant that, in the late 1970s, one in four Coventry workers was directly or indirectly dependent upon the state for his job. But, Coventry would cope; when Jeremy Seabrook visited the city in 1977,[6] he found most Coventrians more preoccupied with material affluence than anything else, with the prospect of decline only distantly perceived.

In 1980, the city's industrial base began to collapse. BL's nationalisation programme led to the closure of its plant at Canley (5,500 jobs), and the loss of 1,600 jobs at the Jaguar factory as well as a further 250 at the Climax works. This job-cutting was, of course, a condition of continued government aid to the company. On the government's insistence, the National Enterprise Board sold the Alfred Herbert firm to a private company, which made redundancies (which eventually totalled 900) a condition of purchase. Talbot (formerly Chrysler and now part of the Peugeot group) found itself in difficulties because the high level of interest rates had reduced demand for its cars and a contract with Iran was suspended because of the revolution, and began to make some of its white-

[5] M. J. Hill, R. M. Harrison, A. V. Sargeant and V. Talbot, *Men Out of Work* (Cambridge U.P., 1973).
[6] J. Seabrook, *What Went Wrong?* (Camelot, 1978).

STAN TAYLOR

collar workers redundant (160 jobs). The problems of these major firms meant the contraction or closure of many minor firms, like Coventry Hood and Seating (120 jobs), Coventry Radials (230 jobs) and Renolds (900 jobs). These losses, added to the lack of jobs for school-leavers, raised the rate of unemployment from 6 per cent. in January 1980 to 10·9 per cent. in September; numerically the increase was from 11,000 to 20,000.

Redundancy

The impact of unemployment in Coventry varied considerably between those put out of a job and those seeking their first one. A joke going the rounds of the Coventry clubs and pubs was that it was easy to spot those workers who had been made redundant; they were the ones in the new suits buying the rounds of drinks. While this somewhat overstates the case (sales in pubs in Coventry decreased by 7 per cent. over 1980), it does illustrate the point that the redundant were at least temporarily cushioned from the bread-line. BL in particular paid well above minimum legal payments to those it made redundant, and in some cases gave 90 days' pay in lieu of statutory notice in addition. A few thousand pounds and earnings-related benefit would see many of the recently unemployed through perhaps a year or 18 months, after which poverty would begin to bite. The spending of redundancy money helped to maintain the local retailing economy, if not at its previous levels. Shops in Coventry's modern city centre precinct did not close through lack of business; the main sign of depression was that the sales began in June in 1980. In the affluent days, they did not begin until September when the car workers had returned broke from their holidays in the sun. Business in the city also held up because of the way in which price cuts benefited the employed; lower prices enabled those in work to buy more, *i.e.* increased the real income available to them for spending.

Sales were not the only sign of depression in the centre of Coventry. A few years ago, the only people in the precinct on weekdays were mothers taking their children to do the shopping. In 1980, these were joined by groups of youngsters mooching around, peering in the shop windows, or occasionally letting off steam by running around and whooping to the general terror of passers-by. Coventry, like the rest of the West Midlands, had an unusually large number of school-leavers coming on to the labour market in 1979 and 1980. In June 1979, 18 per cent. of 16- to 18-year-

70

olds in Coventry were looking for a permanent job; by June 1980, the figure was a staggering 46 per cent. Of the 14,500 school-leavers in 1979 and 1980, over 7,000 were without work. Their prospects of obtaining work in the near future were virtually nil. In September 1980, the Job Centre in Coventry had been notified of 658 vacancies over the city as a whole, of which one-third were suitable for school-leavers.

" Ska " and " Two-Tone "

The frustration of youngsters brought up at a time when Coventry was one of the most affluent cities in Britain and yet who were denied a job, let alone a high wage, was expressed in a variety of ways. One of them was crime. It was hardly coincidental that court appearances by juveniles in Coventry rose by over 20 per cent. between mid-1979 and mid-1980 at the same time as unemployment among the young increased by 27 per cent. Another manifestation of youthful unemployment was the development of a youth culture epitomised by the " Coventry ' rude boys ' ". The " rude boy " was announced by his crew-cut hair, distinctive dress and cultivated expression of dumb insolence; as the name implies his distinctive pose was leaning against a wall hurling insults at passers-by. The brittleness and bitterness of the lives of the rude boys was expressed in their " new wave " music. The songs of Coventry groups such as the " Specials " and " Selector " poured out the plight of the young and were responsible for something of a revolution in British popular music. The success of these groups stemmed in part from the only encouraging aspect of unemployment among the young, its transcendence of differences between whites and blacks. The common experience of unemployment brought young black and young white together and the gangs of " rude boys " were often multi-racial in composition, as were their musical groups. The " Coventry sound " combined punk and West Indian reggae and the lyrics of songs often included protests against racism.

The voices of their musicians were almost the only ones raised on behalf of the Coventry young. Because they had never had the opportunity to work, they were not members of trade unions which might defend their interests. While the Labour Party, particularly the militant-dominated Labour Party Young Socialists, made efforts to incorporate the young into the Labour movement, this was not particularly successful in the face of widespread apathy, or indeed the divisive response of the Labour Party in Coventry to the current economic and political situation. In the late 1970s the Left in the form of Tribunites or supporters of the " Militant Tendency " were able to take over a number of Coventry ward parties to the extent that in the 1979 local elections they were able to force several moderate sitting councillors to stand down and replace them with their own nominees.

In-Fighting on the Council

In 1980, council meetings became a battleground between the Right and Left of the ruling Labour group. One of the central points of disagreement was how far the local authority should obey government instructions to cut expenditure, given the deteriorating employment situation in Coventry. The moderates argued that, however reprehensible it was to socialist principles, the law had to be obeyed : the Left was in favour of making no cuts at all. The disagreement eventually came to a head over the decision of the moderates to increase school meal charges, which the Left voted against. Following this, the Labour whip was withdrawn from them. The image of a divided party was not helped by in-fighting for control of the city party between the two factions. At one meeting early in 1980, the Left took most of the offices but a successful appeal by the Right led to a National Executive ruling that the meeting would have to be held again. At the new meeting, the Left gained control of most of the party offices in the city. With the Labour Party thus engaged, and the unions fully occupied with fighting a rearguard action for their members still in work, little was done for the unemployed. However, in September 1980, the warring factions came together long enough to create a Coventry Labour and Trade Union Campaign for the Unemployed. The aims of this body vary from trying to put pressure on working union members to end overtime, work only a 35-hour week and accept early retirement, to providing free bus passes and entrance to council facilities for the Coventry unemployed. It is unlikely that proposals to share work will find particular favour with union members whose own jobs are threatened; and free bus passes is a less than total answer to de-industrialisation.

Politics and the Future of the West Midlands

The experiences of Coventry were repeated throughout the West Midlands in 1980, albeit on a lesser scale, although it was possible to find instances of higher rates of unemployment (15 per cent. in October in Telford New Town) and odder responses by Labour councils (Walsall announced that it would be unwilling to appoint

Conservatives to jobs involving contact with the public). To be fair, there is a limit to what councils and the Labour movement can do in the West Midlands in face of the fact that the region's skills have not, for the first time in history, proved adequate to expand the industrial base of the region. If the West Midlands is to be saved from becoming an industrial desert, central government intervention on a large scale is required, intervention which goes somewhat beyond the Conservative's sole concession of allowing West Midlands local authorities to bid for a 500-acre " Enterprise Zone ". The government is, of course, resistant on ideological grounds to intervention involving a substantial commitment of public resources. It is possible that, in three years, this may result in a slimmed-down, competitive Britain, but one without either an industrial base in the West Midlands or a Conservative government. The Conservatives did exceptionally well in the West Midlands in the 1979 election. The overall swing to the Conservatives was 6·7 per cent., higher than in any other region except the South East. The swing in the West Midlands conurbation area was 7·1 per cent., greater than in any other Metropolitan conurbation. In the West Midland region, the Conservatives won 10 seats from Labour, seven of which were in the conurbation area. It may well be asked why, in view of subsequent developments, many West Midlanders swung to the Conservatives, why, in the words of a losing Labour candidate explaining his defeat " bloody-minded car workers voted against the interests of bloody-minded car workers ". The answer probably lies in the attractiveness of income tax cuts and free collective bargaining to skilled workers who had suffered from high marginal tax rates and the erosion of differentials by incomes policies. Affluent West Midlanders have always preferred jam today and not worried unduly about tomorrow. But if by 1984 the jam has run out and there is no prospect of any more, the West Midlanders will switch back to Labour. Loss of the 10 West Midland seats and a few others (including car-worker areas such as Oxford and the two Luton seats won from Labour in 1979) would deny Mrs. Thatcher the decade she insists is needed for her policies to work. The threat of the region's Conservative M.P.s joining the swelling ranks of the unemployed may yet persuade the Government to rescue the West Midlands.

SOUTH YORKSHIRE:
THE ECONOMIC AND SOCIAL IMPACT
OF UNEMPLOYMENT

ALAN WALKER

THE purpose of this article is to examine the structure of recent unemployment in South Yorkshire and its impact on the economic and social fabric of the county. Three preliminary points must be made before proceeding with this account. Because analyses of the impact of the present recession in South Yorkshire have only recently begun, it is only possible to make some tentative remarks about the precise nature of the problems created by unemployment for individuals, families and different communities in this region. More considered analyses must await the results of detailed research and inquiry. Secondly, there are major differences between different areas and labour markets *within* South Yorkshire between, for example, the traditionally prosperous city of Sheffield based on manufacturing industry and the long-depressed Dearne valley based on primary industries. The problem of large-scale unemployment is a relatively new experience for Sheffield. Therefore generalisations about the country as a whole are apt to mask important local variations. Thirdly, South Yorkshire, like other industrial areas, forms an integral part of the national and international economy. It may aspire to be the " Socialist Republic of Yorkshire ", with 16 Labour M.P.s to one Conservative and a three-fifths Labour majority on the County Council, but it is unable to prevent the decline in the local economy, which stems from a downturn in world and national demand encouraged by government policies. It is necessary, therefore, to see the problems it faces within the context of broad economic and social changes. One important variable here is the changing attitude of political parties and governments to unemployment.

The recent dramatic increases in the proportion of the population who are unemployed, from 3 per cent. in the early 1970s to 8 per cent. in 1980, have been accompanied by periodically revised projections of both the scale and political implications of unemployment. In fact the politics of unemployment in post-war Britain is

* The author lectures in Social Policy at the University of Sheffield.

marked by three distinct phases. Up to 1966 unemployment averaged 1·8 per cent. of the workforce, and one of the main objectives of Butskellite policies was full employment. One of the key political figures of this period, Macmillan, retained from his experience as M.P. for Stockton-on-Tees in the 1930s, an " instinctive and violent " dislike of the idea of using unemployment as a weapon against inflation.[1] Public opinion polls found that the number unemployed was the most important influence upon the popularity of the Government. In the late 1960s and early 1970s, increases in unemployment under governments of both parties brought renewed commitment to full employment, despite the breaking of the " politically sensitive " half million and one million unemployed barriers in 1967 and 1975, and the maintenance of high levels of unemployment over the lifetime of a Government. The latter part of the 1970s and early 1980s finally saw the death of the post-war consensus on full employment when unemployment reached 1·5 million and then 2 million for the first time in 40 years. Thus the 1979 election meant the end of a Government which had presided over massive increases in unemployment and the accession of one wedded to policies that would inevitably lead to further rises in the numbers out of work. Neither party offered any concrete policy to reduce the level of unemployment. The social costs of this failure of political will and initiative, as well as those resulting from economic changes discussed by Maurice Peston are borne directly by unemployed people and their families and indirectly by the wider community.

The Level and Structure of Unemployment

The most remarkable aspect of recent unemployment is its sheer scale. Unemployment nationally has doubled in the last five years and in the nine months up to October 1980 has risen by over 500,000. Moreover, all reliable predictions indicate that this upward trend will continue. A confidential report to the Department of Industry in 1978 concluded that unemployment of 10–15 per cent. of the workforce was on the cards.[2] The Cambridge Economic Policy Group forecast that unemployment will reach 3 million in the second quarter of 1982.[3] Table 1 shows that the rise in unemployment in South Yorkshire has been no less dramatic than elsewhere. In the space of 18 months unemployment has increased by 35 per

[1] A. Deacon, "Unemployment and Politics in Britain", in B. Showler and A. Sinfield, *The Workless State* (London, Martin Robertson) (forthcoming).

[2] *Financial Times*, November 13, 1978.

[3] Manpower Services Commission, *Manpower Review* (1980), p. 17.

cent., while at the same time (Table 2) vacancies for jobs have fallen by 57 per cent. Both Tables are based on Department of Employment data which understate both the numbers of unemployed, primarily because of the failure of many married women to register, and also the number of vacancies. In addition to the wholly unemployed there are thousands of workers on short-time.

TABLE 1

Unemployment in South Yorkshire December 1978–June 1980

Forecasting Area	Wholly unemployed		Per cent. rate		Per cent. change
	1978	1980	1978	1980	1978–1980
Barnsley	5,383	7,233	6·7	9·0	+ 34·4
Dearne	2,967	3,816	9·8	12·6	+ 28·6
Doncaster	8,297	10,394	7·5	9·4	+ 25·3
Rotherham	5,258	6,799	7·5	9·7	+ 29·3
Sheffield	12,735	18,781	4·3	6·4	+ 47·5
South Yorkshire	34,640	47,023	5·9	8·0	+ 35·7

TABLE 2

Unfilled Vacancies in South Yorkshire December 1978–June 1980

Forecasting Area	Unfilled Vacancies		Unfilled Vacancies as Per cent. Unemployed		Per cent. change
	1978	1980	1978	1980	1978–1980
Barnsley	550	242	10·2	3·3	− 56·0
Dearne	97	50	3·4	1·3	− 48·5
Doncaster	1,028	328	12·4	3·2	− 68·1
Rotherham	275	158	5·2	2·2	− 46·2
Sheffield	1,710	770	13·4	4·1	− 54·4
South Yorkshire	3,660	1,547	10·6	3·4	− 57·7

The recent experience of Sheffield is particularly interesting because the unemployment rate for the city as a whole has been consistently below the national rate since 1950. It was this fact which contributed to the Government's decision to remove the city's assisted area status after 1982. In recent months, however, unemployment in Sheffield has increased at a faster rate than other areas in

South Yorkshire and it looks as though the city will have to live with much higher relative levels of unemployment than it has been used to. Sheffield is the largest population concentration in the county; therefore the *numbers* of unemployed are larger than elsewhere. In contrast Rotherham and especially Dearne have experienced relatively high levels of unemployment for more than 20 years. Between June and August 1980 the unemployment rate in Dearne increased to 14·7 per cent. and Sheffield 7·7 per cent.

There are also important variations in the experience of unemployment between different occupational groups in the labour force. In June 1979 there were two unemployed persons per vacancy in skilled manufacturing, three per vacancy in construction and mining and 82 per vacancy amongst general labourers. In some areas these ratios are even more marked. For example, there are 168 general labourers and miscellaneous workers per vacancy in Mexborough and 189 in Rotherham. Of course, these variations are reflected in the industrial distribution of unemployment and vacancies. In November 1979 there were 13 unemployed for every vacancy in all industries and services, and 21 and 37 respectively in the traditional industries of mining and metal manufacture compared with only seven in services. In the six years between 1973 and 1979 the numbers of unemployed per vacancy in metal manufacturing increased from two to 37.

The Young and Women

In addition to these differences between areas, occupations and industries, the experience of two groups in the labour force, young people and women, deserve particular attention. There has been an upward trend in unemployment amongst those aged under 18 over the last four years. But for females the increase has been 20 per cent. compared with only 1 per cent. for males. Similarly, for those aged 18–19 female unemployment has increased by 72 per cent. compared with 2 per cent. for males. Youth unemployment would have risen even faster had it not been for the Youth Opportunity Scheme. In January 1980, 2,353 places were occupied on schemes in Barnsley, Doncaster, Rotherham and Sheffield. Therefore if these young people are added on to the unemployment statistics, the total of 16–19-year-olds out of work in January 1980 was 9,742, a 60 per cent. increase in unemployment amongst this group in the previous four years compared with 21 per cent. for total unemployment.

Between 1970 and 1980 the unemployment rates for women both nationally and locally have tended to be the same as those for men.

In some areas of South Yorkshire, notably Dearne and Doncaster, female unemployment exceeds that for males. Thus, while there has been a gradual increase in male unemployment, the rise for women has been striking. Between 1970 and 1980 male unemployment doubled while female unemployment increased sixfold. The proportion of school-leavers who are unemployed is far greater in South Yorkshire than the country as a whole, and this is particularly the case amongst women. Over half of the unemployed women in South Yorkshire in July 1979 were under 20 years of age and 70 per cent. were younger than 24. So it is in these age groups that the recent substantial increases in female unemployment have been concentrated. This differential impact of unemployment is likely to have several important social and political consequences.

Unemployment and the Local Economy

There are just over half a million economically active persons in South Yorkshire out of a total population of 1·3 million. The range of industries and services is wide, but the economy revolves around the production of coal and particularly the production and manufacture of steel. Significant differences between the industrial structure of South Yorkshire and Great Britain as a whole stems from the importance of the latter. For example, 10 per cent. of employees in South Yorkshire work in primary industries compared with 3 per cent. in the country as a whole. There is a similar difference in metal manufacture and the production of metal goods. On the other hand, 47 per cent. work in services compared with 59 per cent. in Great Britain. A second and related difference between the industrial structure of South Yorkshire and the country as a whole is the *size* of productive units. Small businesses (less than 100 persons) employ one-fifth of the workforce in South Yorkshire compared with more than two-fifths in Great Britain as a whole. Units of less than 11 persons comprise 45 per cent. of the total manufacturing units compared with 73 per cent. overall. Larger plants are concentrated in the coal industry, metal manufacture, mechanical engineering, electrical engineering, vehicle manufacture and textiles. Therefore, employment depends to a greater extent than it does nationally on heavy industry in large production units, and is therefore particularly vulnerable not only to structural unemployment but also to the results of a more general reduction in demand. In 1976 two-fifths of employees in Sheffield were in manufacturing and two-thirds of these were in two industrial groups: metal manufacture and metal goods. Both aspects of the current unemployment can be seen clearly in Table 1. Rotherham and Dearne have experienced consistently higher levels of unemployment than Sheffield over the last 30 years, but as the recession begins to deepen, normally efficient plants in Sheffield have been forced to declare redundancies or close altogether. Thus, the relative prosperity of Sheffield, compared with other parts of the county, has sheltered it from widespread long-term unemployment and economic and social deterioration of the sort experienced in Dearne. In some parts of the inner city unemployment has been more than 2 per cent. higher than the average for Sheffield. The relative prosperity of Sheffield has been partly based on the production of special steels (carbon steel, alloy steel and stainless steel) and related manufacturing industry. Sheffield and Rotherham form the main special steels centre in the country. The special steels division has been a consistent profit-maker for the British Steel Corporation since 1970 and is its most successful division. The special steel industry, however, is closely related to the manufacture of vehicles (two-thirds of special steel sales in the United Kingdom go to transportation uses) which has been particularly hard hit by imports and the current recession. In addition, the steel industry in Sheffield has suffered from the " dumping " of special steel imports into this country. Frank Hooley, M.P., made the point, in a recent adjournment debate, that imports of high-speed steels had nearly trebled between 1972 and 1978, while over the same period, employment in the special steel sector had fallen by 1,000. In recent months, therefore, parts of Sheffield have begun rapidly to experience the deteriorating economic fabric that has characterised other parts of the country for many years.

As recently as the first quarter of 1979 the slight decline in unemployment nationally and locally, which started the previous year, was continuing in most areas of South Yorkshire with the major exception of Sheffield. This relative short-term change in fortunes was primarily due to the impact of steel imports. This point was emphasised by the Annual Report of the Yorkshire and Humberside Economic Development Planning Council, published in February 1979, which expressed " deep concern " at the rise in unemployment in the region despite the fact that economic performance had been slightly better than the United Kingdom as a whole, and which highlighted the need for government assistance for South Yorkshire's special steel industry and went on to warn of the " imminent collapse of this part of the United Kingdom industry ". At the same time more than 80 redundancies from the Edgar Allen Balfour private steel works were attributed to " dumping ". There were several plant closures in early 1979 as a result of the general depression of the steel industry.

Following the election of the Conservative Government in May 1979 employment prospects nationally and locally became even bleaker. Cuts in industrial investment, local authority expenditure and the freeze on civil service recruitment quickly affected the labour market and employment opportunities in South Yorkshire. Cuts in local authority budgets and in the civil service, as the earlier figures show, had their greatest impact on young women.[4] Female employment was particularly hard hit in areas like Rotherham which lack extensive retail opportunities. Despite the announcement of the go-ahead for the opening of Thorne Colliery and the continuation of a substantial investment programme by the National Coal Board, prospects for the coal industry began to be the worst for many years. The threat of large-scale cheap coal imports and the longer-term move towards nuclear power were chiefly to blame for this apparent change of fortune. Following the announcement of a £300-million loss by British Steel the Industry Secretary, Sir Keith Joseph, insisted that BSC must be in profit by the following year. The losses of £17 per tonne of steel produced, however, compared relatively favourably with other EEC producers, including Belgium with losses of £20 per tonne, Italy £21 per tonne and France £32 per tonne. But the Government took a firm line, and Sheffield alone was asked to save £24 million in the eight months to March 1980. South Yorkshire had lost 1,000 jobs in BSC since January 1977 and considerable job loss resulted from " rationalisation " in the private sector.

By the second quarter of 1980 cuts in public expenditure and the high value of sterling were deepening the impact of the world recession on this country with the result that unemployment was growing at an alarming rate. In the first six months of 1980 3,000 jobs were lost in manufacturing industry in South Yorkshire due to redundancies and closures. In the second quarter of 1980 an additional 1,000 jobs were shed in the steel industry alone. In July and August 1980 twice as many redundancies were declared in Sheffield as in the previous two months, involving some 1,500 people. The annual job loss in Sheffield is around 8,000 jobs.

---

[4] See A. Walker, P. Ormerod and L. Whitty, *Abandoning Social Priorities* (London, CPAG, 1979).

Economic Decline and Regional Policy

In assessing the short- and long-term impact of economic decline, the differences between areas within the county are important. The level of unemployment in some localities, including Goldthorpe and Thorne, is more than *double* the average for the county. Employment prospects in the short and medium term, nationally and locally, are depressing. On the one hand there is increasing labour-market participation on the part of young people born in the early 1960s and married women, and on the other the world recession worsened by government policies. Reduced public financial support for industry means that competition from low-priced imports is likely to add to the damage of recession. Moreover, the scrapping of older plant and machinery has been accelerated in some vulnerable industries. Although recovery is planned for the medium and long term it is difficult to see, with current government policies of reduced industrial investment and lack of action on widespread low-price imports, how industry in South Yorkshire could respond quickly to any stimulus of demand. In the first place, an increasingly large number of factories in the county are closing altogether. Secondly, apart from the National Coal Board, investment has been curtailed. Thirdly, many of those firms which remain open have drastically reduced their recruitment and training. Thus the effects of the current recession and resulting high levels of unemployment will be felt in the long term in South Yorkshire and other relatively deprived regions.

Local statistics on youth employment show the impact of changes in the recruitment policies of firms and demonstrate that the current unemployment is undermining prospects for a future recovery. It is often assumed that unemployment in older industrial regions is concentrated amongst older workers. But despite the traditional nature of industry in South Yorkshire and in particular the importance of mining to the local economy, the proportion of the unemployed who are aged 55 and over is similar to that for Great Britain as a whole (26 per cent. compared to 21 per cent.). A significantly higher proportion than nationally are younger males. Two-thirds of unemployed males in the blackspot Dearne are younger than 55, and one-fifth are under 20. The absence of skill shortages also indicates the deep impact of the recession on South Yorkshire. In the manufacturing centre, Sheffield, there were only 145 skilled vacancies in September 1979 and 230 skilled unemployed. Taken together with the rundown of training and reductions in recruitment to apprenticeships these figures suggest that the recovery of manufacturing industry is likely to be impeded by bottlenecks at some time in the future. At the present time, however, the problem of unemployment is concentrated on the semi-skilled and unskilled.

If the prospects for recovery in the skilled industrial centre of South Yorkshire are bleak, those of the long-devastated areas of Dearne and Rotherham are utterly depressing. The longer the recession continues the worse the prospects for recovery become. Closures and unemployment affect not only the local revenue, but also morale. With falling revenue local services are reduced and morale is, in turn, further depressed. In this climate companies are unlikely to invest in depressed regions with depleted skills and low morale due to long periods of unemployment. Experience in the depressed regions over the last 30 years shows that a phoenix is not likely to rise from the ashes of an industrial wasteland.

The traditional response of governments of both parties to unemployment in the regions has been regional employment policies. It is only a short step, however, from observing variations in unemployment to *explaining* them as " regional " problems. Such explanations of decline arose first in the inter-war depression and resulted in aid for depressed regions. Thus rather than analysing the deprivation of certain local areas within the context of the national distribution of resources and national and international changes in demand and the structure of industry, unemployment and deprivation have been seen as purely local problems.[5] In some areas, notably Merseyside, these problems are identified as being endemic to the area itself. Regional policies have successfully created a large number of jobs in some areas, but the scale of redistribution has been relatively small and the larger centres have tended to dominate expenditure.

In South Yorkshire, Sheffield has benefited most from regional aid, while Doncaster, Mexborough and Goldthorpe have fared relatively poorly. Between 1974 and 1979 Sheffield received roughly three-fifths of South Yorkshire's Regional Development Grant and Rotherham a further 30 per cent. But four-fifths of the total accrued to BSC alone. Without the BSC investment programme South Yorkshire's total grants would have been considerably lower than they were. Once the BSC element has been subtracted the still dominant position of Sheffield is a fairer reflection of the fact that it

[5] A. Walker (ed.), *Rural Poverty: Poverty, Deprivation and Planning in Rural Areas* (London, CPAG, 1978).

supplies over half the job opportunities in South Yorkshire. Other more depressed areas in the county, relying predominantly on mining and metal manufacture, may reasonably feel aggrieved at their lack of success in attracting regional aid, since it is the fact that Sheffield is the most economically buoyant area in the county that is responsible for its receipt of most aid.

Soon after coming to power the Secretary of State for Industry announced a reduction in expenditure on regional aid of £253 million by 1982 (a cut of 40 per cent.). The major change in South Yorkshire was the downgrading of Sheffield from an intermediate area to a non-assisted area. From August 1, 1980, Sheffield no longer qualified for Regional Development Grants. The loss of intermediate area status alone could cost approximately 3,000 jobs in Sheffield. So, although regional aid has failed to reverse the decline of some depressed areas, it has proved significant in Sheffield and therefore in South Yorkshire as a whole in creating jobs. Now that regional aid has been reduced the impact of recession on the economy of the county will be accentuated. The siting of an " enterprise zone " in the inner-city area of Attercliffe is unlikely to reverse this trend.

The Social Division and Impact of Unemployment

While it is relatively simple to identify plant closures and to foresee the longer-term impact of unemployment, falling investment, depreciation of machinery and decline in the skill of the labour force, the social consequences of this decline are more difficult to predict in the absence of detailed research. The use of unemployment as a means of reducing inflation is increasing social divisions, because inflation is borne, albeit differentially, by the whole community while unemployment is carried directly by a much smaller section of society. If unemployment were totally random we could each expect to be out of work seven times during our working lives.[6] Even in periods of relatively full employment the unemployment rate for unskilled workers is more than eight times that for professional workers. The unemployed are more likely than not to have been in low-paid, low-skilled jobs and to come from amongst younger workers, older workers, ethnic minorities and the disabled.[7] Moreover, one in seven of the unemployed are likely to be out of work more than once within a year. All this underlines the fact that unemployment is

[6] R. Lister and F. Field, *Wasted Labour* (London, CPAG, 1978), p. 16.
[7] A. Sinfield, " The Blunt Facts of Unemployment ", *New Universities Quarterly* (Winter, 1979).

closely associated with poverty and low incomes. Thus 84 per cent. of those out of work for three months or more have incomes which do not exceed the poverty line (supplementary allowance scales) by more than 10 per cent., compared with only 4 per cent. of people in work. One of the enduring myths about unemployment is that its link with poverty has been broken. High wages and more two-wage families, it is argued, mean that unemployment today causes little hardship. A recent survey by the DHSS showed to the contrary, that 70 per cent. of men who had been out of work for four or more weeks had no unearned income and no wife's earnings. Furthermore, the degree of concentration of unemployment in Britain amongst those who are already poor and disadvantaged is not found in other countries.[8] These facts make the Government's decisions to uprate unemployment benefit in November 1980 by 5 per cent. less than the rate of inflation and to abolish the earnings-related supplement in 1982 even more difficult to justify.

A study of the Sheffield and Rotherham labour markets identified three groups at particular risk of unemployment and deprivation. Unemployment has grown fastest amongst the unskilled and they now comprise two-fifths of the total. Increasing closures and competition for remaining jobs will further exclude the low-skilled as employers trade-up the skill market. There is little prospect of an improvement in job opportunities in the short or medium term for this group. The combination of low skill and ethnic origin has severely depressed the employment position of those from Pakistan, Bangladesh and the West Indies. These groups are concentrated in manual employment, with women having a generally lower skill level than men. The unemployment rate for those of West Indian, Pakistani and Bangladeshi ethnic origin is more than double that of the white population, and the rate for women is higher than that for men.[9]

Secondly, employment opportunities for young people have been declining rapidly in the past year, despite the increase in temporary employment schemes. A recent decline in retail and clerical work is important here. At the same time the numbers of school-leavers has still to peak in 1981/82. If young people are lucky enough to find work it is very often in a job that is below their educational ability and potential. Thus discontent and alienation amongst some of the employed are likely to be significant factors in addition to the prob-

[8] Supplementary Benefits Commission, *Annual Report 1979* (London, HMSO, 1980).
[9] A. Barber, "Ethnic Origin and the Labour Force", *Employment Gazette* (August 1980), p. 844.

lems created by large numbers of workless young people. The position of young women in the labour market gives particular cause for concern, because in the face of traditional attitudes to working women, they are losing out in competition with men. Young and older women alike are likely to be affected to a greater extent than men by the introduction of new technology and future cuts in public expenditure. Between 1971 and 1976 women lost a slightly higher proportion of jobs in manufacturing industry in Sheffield than men. Jobs in the service sector which attracted large numbers of married women in the 1960s and 1970s are vulnerable not only to changes in government expenditure but also to the introduction of new technology. These trends indicate the need in South Yorkshire as well as nationally for an *expansion* in employment to cater for the increasing numbers of young people and married women seeking work. Even if the current level of economic activity could be maintained, unemployment would increase by the mid-1980s. In the short- and long-term, therefore, unemployment will be a major feature of economic and social life in South Yorkshire.

The impoverishing effects of unemployment on the community is not revealed by the snap-shots provided by statistics. Indeed, these factors are slow to become apparent, and are even more slowly perceived in London and the South-East, where unemployment is relatively low. The findings that are beginning to emerge, as the Supplementary Benefits Commission recently pointed out, are worryingly reminiscent of the 1930s.[10] Long-term unemployment, the shifting of some of the burden of unemployment on to the elderly by premature retirement, families with not only one person out of work, but two or three, are some of the consequences of the deepening recession. It is not only unemployment, but also short-time working, less overtime, more part-time working and widespread bankruptcies amongst the self-employed, which create general reductions in living standards. The financial and emotional stress, depression, boredom, lethargy, loss of status and self-esteem and the paradox of having a great deal of spare time but being unable to participate in customary roles and relationships are the immediate personal and family consequences of unemployment. The experience of unemployment can be demoralising for young people, but when a man or woman with children is affected the hardship is spread over two or more generations and therefore has a long-lasting impact.

[10] SBC, *op. cit.* p. 37.

Family men bear a greater proportion of unemployment in Britain than other EEC countries except Ireland and Denmark. The unemployed are further disadvantaged in the search for work since employers take into account length of time unemployed and many regard long-term unemployment as an indication of unsuitability for work. Research in the United States indicates that unemployment is related to sickness and premature death.[11]

The wider social implications of these costs are just beginning to be discerned and discussed in South Yorkshire and Sheffield in particular. Increases in crime and vandalism may be related to unemployment, especially among young people and more and more young people can be expected to leave the area. Increasing personal stress, family tension and marital conflict create demands on the social services. On the other hand, services are under threat, not only from cuts in public expenditure but also from falling rate revenue due to closures and bankruptcies. Government policies have, in effect, ensured that the unemployed are under constant pressure and that social services are not fully equipped to make an adequate response. Budgets have been cut when there is increasing pressure on the social services and a need for increased expenditure. For example, in Sheffield public expenditure cuts have delayed slum clearance and council building and have added housing stress to the problem of low incomes for some families. Nationally, the direct economic cost of unemployment is substantial. Each 100,000 persons unemployed cost £110 million in benefits and the loss of revenue doubles this cost.

As the recession deepens, facilities in both the public and private sectors have declined. This deterioration is evident in areas like Dearne in the demise of shops and community facilities following the closure of factories, and is likely to become increasingly evident throughout the region as unemployment spirals. Moreover, if unemployment continues to rise at its current rate for much longer, it is certain that some families will be scarred for life by the experience and the South Yorkshire economy as a whole may never fully recover.

Conclusion

Apart from some small inner-city areas the main population centres of South Yorkshire have not hitherto in the post-war period experienced high levels of unemployment. Now Sheffield, like the long-depressed areas of Dearne and Rotherham, will have to adjust to the

---

[11] DHSS, *Inequalities in Health* (1980), p. 163.

wholly new situation of rapidly rising unemployment on a large scale and its social and economic consequences. While the county must attempt to adjust to growing unemployment as quickly as possible, it is dependent like other regions on changes in national economic policy for a major reversal of current trends. The attitude of South Yorkshire to rising unemployment has yet to be clearly spelled out. The political reaction of Sheffield, for which high levels of unemployment are a relatively new experience, will be different from those areas which have been depressed over a long period. As one of the country's most important and productive manufacturing centres with a strong-willed Labour-controlled council, Sheffield is unlikely to be acquiescent in the destruction of its economic and social life by economic policies which are, at best, experimental. The voices of the two groups disproportionately affected by the current unemployment, young people and women, will be added to those of politicians and industrialists in opposition to government policies. Rising unemployment amongst women is particularly significant because the attraction of large numbers of women into employment has, to some extent, changed their economic and political status. The continued use of women as a labour reserve, to be called on or discarded as circumstances demand and legitimated in the use of terms such as " pin-money ", will be increasingly resisted by women themselves. Moreover, as unemployment rises the clear social division between two nations—those with secure employment in white-collar jobs in, say, banking, insurance and the civil service and those in insecure semi-skilled and unskilled jobs—will become more apparent and add to political tensions. The social costs of unemployment and social divisions are primarily borne locally, and in the absence of Government action, South Yorkshire and Sheffield in particular must quickly develop means of channelling the anger and frustration of unemployed people to productive ends and of supporting those out of work in their desire for the right to decent occupation.

THE POLITICS OF UNEMPLOYMENT IN SCOTLAND

STEPHEN MAXWELL

IN the months immediately after the 1979 General Election a favourite pastime of observers of Scottish politics was to count the parallels with Scotland's situation after the 1970 Election. In both elections the Scottish voter, on the rebound from a hectic affair with the SNP, returned a decisive majority of Labour M.P.s—44 out of Scotland's total of 71—only to find himself facing a Conservative Government chosen by English voters. A Conservative Government, moreover, intent on pursuing radical policies which, whatever their boasted long-term merits, were acknowledged even by their champions in Scotland to pose a serious threat to Scottish jobs in the short term.

Mr. Heath came to power, of course, committed to culling the lame ducks of British industry, of which Scotland demonstrably had more than her fair share. Nine years later Mrs. Thatcher came to her task fired by an ideologically more rigorous commitment to cutting back public expenditure, on which Scotland, again, was disproportionately dependent. On both occasions unemployment, which had first risen and then begun to decline under the preceding Labour Governments, began to rise again at an increased rate. And in both cases before the first year was out voices were being raised across the political spectrum in protest at the effect of government policies on Scotland's economic prospects. Beyond the first year, however, the game begins to go sour: the parallels run out. As they peer into the future, few observers of the Scottish scene are rash enough to stake their reputations on Scotland repeating the campaign of resistance which so enlivened Scottish politics between 1971 and 1974.

When the workers of Upper Clyde Shipbuilders led by Clydebank refused in August 1971 to accept closure of the yards, an impressive alliance of Scottish opinion rallied to their support. It was clear that the rebuff inflicted on the SNP and the disappointment suffered by the Labour Party in the General Election had not seriously damaged Scottish morale. In September 1971, just 16 months after being

* The author is a Tutor in Politics at Edinburgh University and member of the National Executive Committee of the Scottish Nationalist Party.

reduced to 11 per cent. of the Scottish vote in the election, the SNP gained 35 per cent. of the vote in the Stirling, Falkirk and Grange-mouth by-election. As unemployment continued to rise from 90,000 in 1970 to the then post-war record of 137,000 in 1973, the Scottish Trades Union Congress (STUC) provided an outlet for Scotland's sense of outrage through its Special Conference on Unemployment in Edinburgh's Usher Hall in February 1972. Scottish businessmen vied with trades union leaders in demanding an alternative economic strategy for Scotland. More embarrassing to the platform party, SNP delegates led a chorus of demands for Scottish control over the Scottish economy and for a Scottish share of the oil wealth recently discovered off Scotland's coast. Then in November 1973, as if to celebrate Scotland's contribution to forcing the Heath Government to make a U-turn in economic policy which had helped to reduce Scottish unemployment below 100,000, the voters of Glasgow Govan delivered that formerly safe Labour seat to the SNP in a by-election.

Political Vacuum

Sixteen months after the election of Mrs. Thatcher's Government there are few signs of a comparable Scottish come-back, in spite of the fact that the election left SNP with 17 per cent. of the vote, a higher base level of support than the Party had enjoyed after the 1970 Election. True, SNP won 26 per cent. of the vote in the Glasgow Central by-election in June and has polled respectable shares of 20 per cent. or more in local government by-elections. But activists and voters seem merely to be going through the motions. In spite of shocking some of the staider elements of Scottish opinion, the SNP's new oil campaign launched in September featuring Mrs. Thatcher as a grinning vampire with her fangs dripping oil under the slogan: "No Wonder She's Laughing—She's Got Scotland's Oil", lacks the resonance of the "It's Scotland's Oil" campaign of the early 1970s.

Nor is the Labour Party able to excite Scottish anger against rising unemployment. In spite of its success in dishing the Nats in the Scottish Assembly Referendum and its subsequent Scottish tri-umph in the General Election, in spite of the unprecedented 45–50 per cent. support it is consistently gaining in opinion polls, it has failed to generate a popular campaign of resistance to the Conserva-tive Government. Its strategy seems to be to concentrate on organis-ing a "Town Hall" revolt against Conservative cuts in the rate support grants and to leave the larger issues like unemployment to look after themselves.

The STUC has so far failed to play the unifying and co-ordinating role between different sections of Scottish opinion which was its major contribution to the encouragement of a militant Scottish resistance to the Heath Government. It convened a conference on unemployment in November but without the publicity build-up which preceded its 1972 conference. And it restricted representation from each of Scotland's political parties to a maximum of 30, perhaps to save itself the embarrassment of a repeat of the near SNP takeover in 1972.

In this political vacuum the only resistance being offered to the wave of redundancies which has lifted Scottish unemployment above 250,000 is rhetorical and symbolic. No one encouraged the 700 workers when under threat of redundancy at Robb Caledon's shipyard in Dundee, where unemployment is at 13 per cent., to emulate their brothers at Upper Clyde Shipbuilders nine years ago. The 3,000 workers at Singers of Clydebank, the 400 workers at that failed saviour of the Highlands, Wiggins Teape's pulp mill at Fort William, the 750 workers at ICI's Ardeer plant, and thousands of other Scots workers facing unemployment, feature briefly in the national Press and on television as their sentence of redundancy is announced, then disappear noiselessly from public ken to reappear only in the decent anonymity of the monthly unemployment figures.

Scottish inactivity under the joint assault of record unemployment figures and predictions of wholesale industrial collapse contrasts oddly with the public demonstrations of Welsh anger at the losses of Welsh jobs. No visiting Government Minister has been mobbed by a crowd of Scottish steel workers as Sir Keith Joseph was mobbed in Wales. No angry contingent of unemployed Scots has shattered the windows of Eton as it marched in protest through English shires. No English-owned holiday cottages in the Highlands have been the targets of arson attacks. No veteran leader of Scottish nationalism has gone on hunger strike to defend a pledged Scottish interest against the fickleness of a newly elected Government.

True, no sector of Scottish industry has suffered so badly from a Government decision as the Welsh steel industry. No issue in Scottish politics packs the symbolic punch of the language issue or the English holiday-home invasion in Wales. On the other hand, the majority vote in the Scottish Assembly Referendum might have been expected to fortify the spirit of resistance, and the Welsh referendum debacle to have undermined Welsh morale. And the Welsh have no issue to fuel their indignation like the swelling Government revenues and private company profits now being drained from North Sea oil.

The weakness of the Scottish political response to the rising levels of unemployment appears to represent a break with the post-war pattern of Scottish politics. The record suggests a rough correlation between rising unemployment and a swing of votes towards the opposition parties. The decline of the Conservative vote in Scotland from its 1955 peak of just over 50 per cent. giving the Conservatives 36 of Scotland's 71 seats, was accompanied by a long-term rise in Scottish unemployment. Between 1955 and 1964 when the Conservatives lost office the Scottish unemployment rate went up from 2·4 per cent. to 3·6 per cent.—hitting 4·8 per cent. (90,000) in 1963—while the Conservative share of the vote fell back to 40·6 per cent. with the Liberals and Labour, and rather more modestly, the SNP, all sharing the spoils. With the Labour Party in government after 1964 SNP's emergence as the main challenger for the role of Scotland's opposition party coincided with fresh increases in unemployment. After falling back to 3 per cent. in the first two years of Labour government, unemployment rose to 3·9 per cent. in the year of SNP's breakthrough at the Hamilton by-election in 1967.

The Main Opposition Party

If unemployment remained high at 3·7 per cent. in 1969 as SNP support began to decline, and even climbed higher to 4·2 per cent. in the year of SNP's election reverse, that serves as a reminder that unemployment cannot be seen as a single and sufficient cause of electoral swings but as one important factor among others whose strength vary with the circumstances. The poor record of some of the SNP councillors returned in the May 1968 local elections when SNP support was at its peak of 36 per cent., Labour's counter-attack on the economics of independence in publications like South Ayrshire M.P. Jim Sillars' pamphlet " Don't Let the Nats Butcher Scotland's Future " which argued that SNP policies would themselves lose Scotland thousands of jobs, perhaps simply the fading of SNP's novelty appeal, no doubt have a part to play in explaining SNP's decline in 1969 and 1970.

In any event, the correlation between rising unemployment and a swing to " opposition " voting in SNP's favour quickly reappears after the 1970 Election. As Scottish unemployment began its rise from 90,000 in 1970 at the beginning of Mr. Heath's term of office, the SNP, benefiting perhaps from Labour's recent failures on the employment issue when in government, began to emerge again as a major challenger for Scotland's opposition vote. This time the momentum of resentment created by the new record levels of unemployment reached in 1971 and 1972 carried the Nationalists to 21·9 per cent. of the vote in the February Election of 1974 and 30·4 per cent. in the Election of October as the Conservative vote slumped from 38 per cent. in 1970 to 24·7 per cent. in October, and Labour stagnated at 36 per cent.

SNP's role as the main opposition Party was reinforced by the return of a Labour Government in February 1974 and the relegation of the Conservatives to third-party status. As unemployment began to rise again under the Labour Government, SNP improved its electoral standing still further in opinion polls and in a series of local government by-elections in 1975 and 1976. If the momentum of the SNP advance had begun to weaken by February 1978 when unemployment topped 200,000 for the first time in Scotland since the 1930s, it was still strong enough to produce a 3·6 per cent. swing to the SNP in the Glasgow Garscadden by-election of March 1978, though not strong enough to bring the SNP victory. As unemployment began to fall below 200,000, SNP support began the long decline which left it with 30 per cent. of the vote in its former stronghold of Hamilton in the by-election of May 1978 and 17 per cent. in the General Election of May 1979 when unemployment had fallen to 170,000.

Such attempts to explain Scottish electoral developments as a response to the fluctuations of unemployment around a rising trend have a rough plausibility. But they have defects, too. If SNP's emergence in the late 1960s can be explained as a response to the opening created for an alternative party of Scottish opposition by Labour's transference to office and its disappointing record on unemployment between 1966 and 1970, it fails to provide a convincing explanation of SNP's grass-roots growth in the late 1950s and early 1960s when Labour's reputation was unstained by a period of recent government. Conversely, and more important for our purposes, it fails to explain Labour's success in re-establishing itself as the party of Scottish opposition in the face of the employment record of the Labour Government and the failure of the Labour Party in opposition since the 1979 Election to protect Scottish jobs against Conservative policies.

Has unemployment been neutralised as a political issue in Scotland? Must we abandon the plausible theory that movements in the level of unemployment are key factors in determining Scotland's political responses? Following the experience of run-away inflation in 1975/76, opinion polls revealed that unemployment was being displaced by inflation as the main worry of British voters. Separate polls of Scottish opinion carried out in those years confirmed that Scottish opinion followed the changes of British opinion after a slight delay. Separate polls of Scottish priorities have not been available on a regular basis since 1979 but if Scottish opinion has continued to reflect British opinion, unemployment will again be challenging inflation as the most urgent Scottish issue. It is, of course, a familiar irony of British politics that in an economy in which it appears impossible to get prices and unemployment moving downwards at the same time, the more successful a Conservative Government is in achieving its traditional aim of controlling inflation, the more the public worries about unemployment: and the more a Labour Government succeeds in its traditional aim of reducing unemployment, the more public concern is redirected towards inflation.

Hardship

A second explanation for the neutralisation of unemployment as a political issue is the spreading belief that unemployment no longer imposes serious financial hardships. This belief has its roots in popular misconceptions about the scope and generosity of welfare benefits, and was probably reinforced by the Redundancy Payments Act of 1965 and the subsequent publicity given to the size of redundancy payments made to some long-term workers in some industries. The level of unemployment benefits has improved since the 1930s, relatively as well as absolutely. But they remain modest enough—£33·50 for a married man with two children compared to the average male manual wage of £93·06. It is therefore not surprising that in 1978 in Scotland 10,000 unemployed in receipt of unemployment benefits were also eligible for supplementary benefits. With the continued growth of long-term unemployment, the cut in the real value of unemployment benefits from November and the elimination at the beginning of 1982 of the earnings-related benefit, the number is bound to increase.

Many unemployed meanwhile receive no redundancy payments. Only 47 per cent. of a sample of 2,300 unemployed surveyed by researchers from the Department of Employment in 1978 received any special payment on losing their jobs, and of those three-fifths received less than £100. Among other factors, the rising number of the young unemployed has meant that a growing proportion of the unemployed are ineligible for unemployment benefit. In Scotland in 1978 no fewer than 70,000 out of a total registered unemployed of 169,000 were eligible only for supplementary allowance, compared to 28,000 out of a total of 98,000 in 1970. Although supplementary benefit rates increased at twice the rate of the retail price index between 1948 and 1979 and up to 8 per cent. faster than average earnings (depending on the size of the recipient's family), the supplementary allowances received by a man with four children represented only 54 per cent. of average male manual wages in 1979.

The erroneous belief that unemployment no longer imposes a serious financial hardship is cousin to the belief that the changing composition of the unemployed population reduces the social and psychological tragedy of unemployment. In Scotland in December 1979, 58,000 of the total 170,000 Scottish unemployed were women compared to 19,000 out of 98,000 10 years earlier, an increased share which reflects not only the rising proportion of women in the labour force but a rising rate of job losses for women caused partly by the closure of many of the assembly-type operations established by multinational companies in the United States' investment boom of the 1960s and partly by cuts in public service jobs. In the year to January 1980 the largest proportionate increase in Scottish unemployed took place among women in the 25–44 age group.

The increase in the proportion of young people in the unemployed population has been equally striking. In 1971 33,000 of the total 104,000 male unemployed were under 25, less than a third. In 1980 (January) 46,000 out of the total male unemployed of 132,000 were under 25, significantly more than a third. Among women the increase was comparable. In 1971 13,000 of the 25,000 unemployed Scots women were under 25. By 1980 no fewer than 37,000 out of the total 71,000 were under 25, with the greatest increase occurring among the under-18 age group.

It is probably true that except for those women who are single parents—a rapidly growing group in Scotland as elsewhere—unemployment among women has fewer financial consequences than unemployment among men, if only for the reason that women's wages are so much lower than men's. And given the persistence of sexual type-casting it may be the case that women still suffer less in psychological and emotional terms from unemployment than do men. But any tendency to public complacency about unemployment arising either from misconceptions about the financial position of the unemployed or from the presumed consequences of the changing sexual composition of the unemployed is surely outweighed by the widespread guilt at the number of young people unable to find work—27,000 under 19 years in Scotland in 1979 and another 18,000 under 25. If unemployment has been neutralised as a political issue it is not because the public has come to believe that unemployment does not matter.

Expectations

A fourth and more convincing explanation of the changing impact of unemployment on recent Scottish politics may be found in the decline of economic expectations. It would not be surprising if the constant reiteration by successive Governments, backed by the media, that the nation was living beyond its means had persuaded the public that a drop in living standards was inevitable. A high level of unemployment may have come to be accepted as an unavoidable consequence of the United Kingdom's economic decline or a necessary condition of economic recovery, or perhaps as both one and the other.

There are good reasons why a collapse of expectations should have reduced SNP support while helping to consolidate the Labour Party's dominance in Scotland. From its emergence in the late 1960s as a serious challenger to the established parties in Scotland, SNP was able to attract disproportionate support from the young voter in general and the young skilled worker in particular, and from the Scottish New Towns. Indeed, at the peak of its strength in the mid-1970s SNP attracted a higher level of support from skilled workers and trade union members in the 18–34 age group than did the Labour Party, and its popularity in the New Towns was demonstrated by its control of Cumbernauld Council from 1968 virtually through to 1978, a period of control in East Kilbride between 1977 and 1979 and disproportionate, if short-lived successes in Glenrothes in 1968 and in Livingston and Irvine in the 1970s.

SNP's emphasis on Scotland's potential for economic growth rather than on the traditional class objectives of the Labour Party made it particularly attractive to the ambitious, socially mobile, skilled Scot eager to escape from the stagnation of Scotland's older urban and industrial areas in which, perhaps, he had been brought up. The climax of SNP's appeal as the party of " rising expectations " came with the oil campaign of the 1970s which offered a politically and economically painless route to Scandinavian prosperity and classlessness. It is, of course, impossible to provide independent and direct confirmation of SNP's appeal as the Party of " rising expectations ". The only evidence is indirect or circumstantial.

The rate of wage increases is perhaps the only quantifiable evidence which may throw light on the state of economic expectations. It may be assumed that wage demands reflect some judgment, however rudimentary, of the economy's capacity to support higher living standards. There is no significant correlation between the rate of wage increases for manual workers—a rate which corresponds closely to the increase in average earnings for all groups—and the swing of the Scottish vote away from the party of government between the mid-1950s and the mid-1960s. But the acceleration in the rate of wage increases from 1967 coincides with SNP's first appearance as a major force in Scottish politics. The rate of wage increases declines slightly in 1969 as SNP support ebbs, before accelerating from 1970 to reach record rates in the period 1974–77, the peak of SNP's oil campaigning as of its electoral popularity. It is interesting to note that in spite of the misgivings of some of the more traditional elements in the Party, the SNP publicly supported the miners in the confrontation with the Heath Government over wages which led to the Election of February 1974. And it may also be relevant that over this period Scottish wage rates for skilled labour caught up with, and even in some cases overtook, United Kingdom rates. Meanwhile prices, while accelerating, lagged behind wage increases. Then as the rate of wage increases began to decline under Callaghan's non-statutory incomes' policies and price inflation receded from its 1975/76 peak, SNP faltered in the Garscadden by-election of April 1978, stumbled badly in the Hamilton by-election and the Regional Elections of May, and fell heavily in the General Election the following year.

The defects of any single-cause explanation for this lack of protest are demonstrated again by the failure of SNP support to revive in response to the wage and price explosion which followed the new Government's purist rejection of incomes' and prices' policies. It may be that the wage increases were largely a defensive response to the price inflation brought about by the early budgetary and economic decisions of the new Government. Or it may be that the persistence of high unemployment accompanied by the constant threat of further increases was breaking the established patterns of political response.

Although rising unemployment in the post-war period may have persuaded voters to support the most credible among the opposition parties, the pre-war record is more ambiguous. The 1920s were a miners in the confrontation with the Heath Government over decade of deepening economic crisis. As the post-war boom collapsed, Scottish unemployment rose well above 100,000. They were also years of sensational progress by the Labour Party as it replaced the fragmented Liberals as the main Scottish opposition party, raising its share of the vote from 32 per cent. in 1922 with 29 seats to 42 per cent. in 1929 with 36 seats. But as the economic crisis intensified and Scottish unemployment rose above 200,000 towards the end of the decade, the radical mood gave way to a wave of conservatism. In the 1931 Election MacDonald's National Government won 64 per cent. of the Scottish vote and the Labour Party with 32 per cent. of the vote had its parliamentary representtion cut to seven. In 1935 when Scottish unemployment was over 30 per cent. the National Government held nearly 50 per cent. of the vote, against 41 per cent. for the Labour Party. If the fear of unemployment played a part in securing 48 per cent. of the vote for Labour in the next Election in 1945 it was unemployment remembered from the economic security of war-time full employment.

A similar swing to conservatism may be behind the changed political impact of unemployment today. Only it is the Labour Party not the Conservative Government which is reaping the electoral benefits in Scotland. That is less Irish than it sounds. The Labour Party has enjoyed a parliamentary majority in Scotland now for 21 years. In many areas it has been the established party of local government for several decades. If it has not been notably successful in protecting Scotland from the economic ills of the United Kingdom—Scottish unemployment, for example, has increased from 90,000 to 250,000 during Labour's Scottish regnum—it has, at least, to adapt a phrase which Edinburgh historian Nicholas Philipson has used to describe the nationalism of Sir Walter Scott, pursued a strategy of noisy inaction. In other words, it has made most of the right noises. To voters looking for reassurance in a time of growing economic insecurity the Labour Party offers itself as a familiar and trusted champion of the working people of Scotland. No matter that the champion's eye is dim, his arm weak, and his armour rusty. No one expects him to ride out to seek battle. In the current mood familiar rhetoric is more acceptable than radical action leading who knows where.

Yet the ease with which the Scots have been persuaded over the last two years to abandon the high expectations of the mid-1970s remains a puzzle. Against the background of North Sea oil it suggests a chronic lack of collective confidence. The economic logic of the Nationalist case is not weaker today than it was five years ago. Indeed, with annual production from the Scottish sector now heading for 100 million tons, it is stronger than ever. When challenged directly, the majority of Scots will still say, as they were saying five years ago, that Scotland has a special claim on the oil revenues. But the faith that oil can radically alter Scotland's economic prospects has gone, destroyed not by a catastrophic fall in the price of oil, or by the discovery of cheap alternatives, or even by a counter-attack on the Nationalists' oil argument by their political opponents, but simply by the demonstration under both Labour and Conservative Governments that North Sea oil offers no panacea for Britain's economic ills and by the consequent decline of Scottish expectations within the British framework which the Nationalists themselves reject.

The Impact of Unemployment

The social and psychological impact of unemployment rising towards 300,000 will be registered first by an increase in the incidence of poverty in Scotland. Already one in five Scots lives on or within 40 per cent. of the supplementary benefit rate: some estimates put the figure as high as one in four. From recent experience it is clear that the 70,000 increase in unemployment over the last 16 months will force another 30,000 people with their families to turn to supplementary benefits. Forthcoming cuts in unemployment benefits will increase the numbers of those dependent on supplementary rates still further. The young and the over-25s will be the main victims along with women and the unskilled. Throughout Scotland communities like Alexandria with 16 per cent. unemployment, the Lanarkshire town of Lanark where there is an 18 per cent. rate, Bo'ness in West Lothian with 11 per cent., Cumnock in Ayrshire with 15 per cent., and Glasgow with 14 per cent., will all have to carry a heavier burden of depressed and demoralised citizens. The defensiveness of the Scottish character will be confirmed and the chances of reform of Scottish institutions and economy will be further weakened.

The cultural effect of a return to the mass-unemployment level of the pre-war decades is likely to be as damaging as the social and psychological effect. Industrialisation was a harsh experience in Scotland even by the standards of the 19th century, with punitive Poor Laws, poor housing, generally lower wages than south of the border and a mass influx of Irish and Highland immigrants. Then in the Depression Scotland's high level of dependence on trade made Scotland particularly vulnerable to the fall in world trade. For the politically active working class the suffering caused by economic decline was compounded by the humiliation of political defeats in 1919, 1926 and 1931.

The process of de-industrialisation in the latter part of the 20th century threatens to be hardly less demoralising to Scotland than industrialisation in the 19th. Except for the war and post-war booms the Scottish economy has been in relative decline since the 1920s, the worst hit being the Scottish capital industries—steel-making, shipbuilding, engineering and, of course, mining. Since 1964 employment in mining (excluding oil) has declined by 36,000, in shipbuilding and marine engineering by 11,000, metal manufacture by 18,000 and mechanical engineering by 30,000. In the last 10 years alone Scotland has lost 100,000 manufacturing jobs, and the service industries, expanding more slowly than in most Western developed countries, have been unable to provide the jobs needed. In a major world recession even emigration, that traditional way of resisting accommodation to declining expectations, may be limited. There is a real danger that the return of mass unemployment will imprint ever more firmly on Scotland a culture of despair which will kill all hope or will for reform.

UNEMPLOYMENT AND WAGES IN NORTHERN IRELAND

N. J. GIBSON AND J. E. SPENCER

NORTHERN Ireland has had a persistent and serious unemployment problem since the foundation of the state some 60 years ago. With the exception of the period of the Second World War, registered unemployment has never averaged less than 5 per cent. and has generally been markedly in excess of this figure. In September 1980 it was 15·5 per cent. (including school-leavers) and is expected to rise further. In addition, the average duration of unemployment has risen substantially in recent years. The recorded incidence of unemployment has mostly been much greater amongst men than women. However, there is reason to believe that if allowance was made for the under-reporting of female unemployment, the rates of unemployment for the two sexes would be similar.[1] The under-reporting in part occurs because women married before April 1980 are not obliged to pay Class I National Insurance Contributions and thereby do not qualify for unemployment or sickness benefit, which gives them little incentive to register as unemployed.

Within Northern Ireland the distribution of unemployment is highly variable. At the September 1980 count, Strabane, Newry Dungannon and Cookstown each had an unemployment rate of more than 25 per cent. However, between them they accounted for only 13·6 per cent. of total unemployment in N. Ireland, whilst the Belfast travel-to-work area had 43·5 per cent. of the total. Yet the Belfast area had an unemployment rate of 12·7 per cent. or about half the rate for the four areas mentioned. But within the Belfast area the rates also vary with rates well in excess of 30 per cent. occurring in west Belfast. Putting aside areas such as west Belfast the heaviest unemployment rates occur in the north-west, west and south of Northern Ireland or broadly speaking west of the river Bann—a fact of political as well as economic and social significance

The heaviest unemployment rates are found amongst processing construction and transport operations and the lowest amongst the managerial and professional and the clerical and related categories

---

* The authors are Professors of Economics in the New University of Ulster.
[1] See Janet M. Trewsdale, *Unemployment in Northern Ireland 1974–79* (Northern Ireland Economic Council, No. 14, September 1980).

The last two cover many who ordinarily work in the public sector. Unemployment is also concentrated amongst the relatively unskilled and amongst married men with large families; indeed the two latter categories overlap markedly. There is also reason to believe that the unemployed experience relatively more sickness than the population as a whole.

Historically, unemployment in Northern Ireland is linked to that in Great Britain. It is, of course, to be expected that fluctuations in economic activity in Great Britain will be reflected in the Northern Ireland economy, because of the well-known and extensive dependence of the latter on Great Britain as a market for exports and, more broadly, because Northern Ireland is directly subject to United Kingdom Government fiscal, monetary and other policies and to many other wage and price influences which spread their effects throughout the whole United Kingdom economy. On these grounds alone Northern Ireland has a powerful vested interest in both the scale and growth of economic activity in Great Britain and in the economic and other policies of central government.

Labour Market Influences

Unemployment is the outcome of the complex interactions of the supply of and the demand for labour. Though these interactions as they affect the Northern Ireland economy are far from being fully understood it is possible to distinguish some of the key factors involved. One of the important ones on the supply side of the labour market is the natural rate of increase of the population which in time has a bearing on the numbers seeking employment. For many years the natural rate of increase has been greatly in excess of that for the United Kingdom as a whole and for 1978 the respective rates per 1,000 of the population were 6·6 and 0·4. However, the increase in population has been much reduced because of migration and in recent years entirely eliminated by it. Between 1961 and 1971 the population increased by almost 8 per cent. but from then until 1974 there was only a slight increase and since then there has been a small decline. Over the period 1971 to 1978 births exceeded deaths by 88,000, thus representing a high annual migration rate of some 7·1 per 1,000 of the population.

Another factor influencing the supply of labour is the growing numbers of females seeking both part and full-time employment. This is in part reflected in the actual numbers in employment which

TABLE 1

Employees in Employment in Major Industrial Groups. Selected Years.
June of Each Year.

Year	Total No.	Primary No.	%	Manufacturing No.	%	Construction No.	%	Private Services[1] No.	%	Public Services[1] No.	%
1959	437,479	23,677	5.4	173,550	39.7	38,623	8.8	98,734	22.6	102,895	23.5
1960	449,285	22,521	5.0	181,282	40.3	36,671	8.2	100,568	22.4	108,243	24.1
1970	486,229	15,774	3.2	177,481	36.5	45,806	9.4	110,841	22.8	136,327	28.0
1975	497,067	12,121	2.4	155,793	31.3	40,384	8.1	102,731	20.7	186,038	37.4
1979 [2]	513,650	11,000	2.1	140,100	27.3	37,550	7.3	118,000	23.0	207,000	40.3

Source: DMS Gazette, No. 1 (Spring 1978) and No. 3 Issue (1979).
  [1] For the years 1959, 1960 and 1970 Private Services are defined to include SIC Orders XXIII, XXIV and XXVI and Public Services the remaining Orders. For 1975 and 1979 Public Services is Public Sector Civil Employment as produced by DMS and Private Services is a residual from the total for service industries. The figures in Table 1 for the years before 1975 probably understate Public Services employment by about 5 per cent. and correspondingly overstate Private Services.
  [2] Provisional.

grew from 157,000 in 1959 to 225,000 in 1979, an increase of 43 per cent. whilst the number of males in employment was almost static having risen from 281,000 in 1959 to 303,000 in 1970 with a subsequent fall by 1979 to 288,000.

Many diverse factors have also been at work on the demand side of the labour market. Perhaps the most striking long-term effects are implicit in the major shifts that have taken place over the last 20 years in the industrial classification of employment. Some selected figures may be seen in Table 1.

Employment in the primary sector, predominantly agriculture, has continued its long-established decline with the number of employees falling by over 50 per cent. during the last 20 years; and, in addition, the number of self-employed in this sector has also fallen greatly. Employment in manufacturing industry, after some fluctuation in the 1960s, has declined markedly during the 1970s and now constitutes some 27 per cent. of the number of employees, having reached a peak of over 40 per cent. in 1960. The shipbuilding and engineering industry had 24,000 employees in 1960; by 1979 the number was 8,700; the corresponding figures for textiles are 58,000 and 30,000; for clothing and footwear 26,000 and 19,000. In fact, each of the standard industrial classification orders which in 1960 accounted for a sizeable proportion of employment in the manufacturing sector has declined substantially in terms of numbers employed during the last 20 years. These declines reflect, at least in part, strong shifts in demand for labour.

Notwithstanding the large reductions in employment in the primary and manufacturing sectors, Table 1 shows that total employment has increased. The source of this increase lies in the service industries; and the major part of the increase is in the public sector. Over the 20 years 1959 to 1979 a remarkable expansion of employment in the public services has taken place with the numbers employed rising by about 100,000—*i.e.* an approximate doubling over the 20 years. In 1959 some 25 per cent. of total employees were in the public sector; by 1979 there was over 40 per cent.—a figure much in excess of the 31 per cent. (for 1978) for the United Kingdom.

The major structural shifts that would seem to have occurred in the demand for labour raise questions about the whole approach to regional policy over the past 20 years. This matter and the related one of the extreme dependence of the Northern Ireland economy on the public sector and hence on public expenditure are taken up below.

TABLE 2

Northern Ireland Average Gross Weekly Earnings as Percentages of Great Britain, April 1971–April 1979. Full-time Adults.

	1971	1972	1973	1974	1975	1976	1977	1978	1979
Men Aged 21 and Over:									
Manufacturing	87·3	87·0	87·5	89·6	91·7	95·4	90·1	92·4	93·1
All Industries	87·6	87·8	88·3	89·4	90·0	95·5	91·7	91·5	92·1
Women aged 18 and Over:									
Manufacturing	88·4	91·1	91·0	88·4	92·3	97·8	94·6	96·5	92·3
All Industries	91·3	92·2	92·4	94·7	94·9	99·5	98·4	98·1	98·1

Source: DMS Gazette, No. 3 Issue (1979).

Wages and Incomes

If, as it would seem, there have been powerful influences operating on the supply and demand for labour it is perhaps not surprising in a world of incomplete information, uncertainty about the future and probably large costs of movement and adjustment that unemployment should be such a persistent problem in Northern Ireland. But the question remains, what has been happening to wages and incomes and, in particular, to what extent have wages been a factor making for equilibrium in the labour market.

Data from the New Earnings Survey, available for each April since 1971, indicate that since then average gross weekly earnings of full-time adult employees have moved closer to those in Great Britain, as may be seen in Table 2.

In 1971 earnings for men were some 87 per cent. of those in Great Britain and by 1979 the figure had risen to around 92 or 93 per cent. For women earnings in manufacturing have risen from some 88 per cent. in 1971 to 92 per cent. in 1979 of those in Great Britain, whilst for all industries, which is strongly weighted by the expanding service industries and especially by the public sector, the corresponding figures are 91 per cent. and 98 per cent.

Thus, since 1971 despite the much heavier unemployment in Northern Ireland than in any other parts of the United Kingdom wages have risen relatively to those in Great Britain, though in absolute and nominal terms they remain somewhat lower, especially for men. Since prices have moved similarly between Great Britain and Northern Ireland real wages in Northern Ireland must have grown relatively to those in Great Britain. Many factors have brought this about, probably the most important being the combined influences of the trade union policy of parity of wage rates with those in Great Britain for comparable occupations and the expansion of the service industries, notably in the public sector which almost automatically extends British wages and salaries to Northern Ireland. On one level the growth in wages and salaries relatively to those in Great Britain is no doubt admirable for the fortunate recipients but on another it may, alas, accentuate the unemployment problem and encourage migration.

Though wages and salaries for comparable occupations may be similar or even identical with those in Great Britain, income per capita is substantially less. Many forces operate to bring this about including a different occupational structure, relatively heavy unemployment and a higher proportion of dependants in the population.

TABLE 3

Expenditure and Value Added Per Capita
Northern Ireland and United Kingdom. Selected Years. (£)

	1966		1970		1974		1978	
	N.I.	U.K.	N.I.	U.K.	N.I.	U.K.	N.I.	U.K.
Expenditure (Market Prices):								
Private Consumption	346	446	474	573	753	931	1,506	1,721
Public Consumption	115	119	157	162	429	296	799	586
Personal Investment	16	20	20	23	42	39	79	99
Business Investment	63	77	87	103	150	175	251	306
Government Investment	26	31	41	44	56	78	71	79
Total Expenditure	566	693	779	905	1,431	1,519	2,706	2,790
Value Added (Factor Cost):								
Agriculture	39	19	43	22	62	36	107	67
Industry	188	285	216	360	366	540	687	1,057
Construction	39	42	56	55	87	107	193	154
Private Services	98	202	176	262	266	453	491	862
Government Services	56	69	84	97	213	188	391	359
Total Value Added	420	618	575	797	994	1,323	1,870	2,498
Indirect Taxes *less* subsidies	54	89	79	136	89	151	186	347
Total Value Added (Market Prices)	474	707	655	933	1,083	1,474	2,056	2,845
Regional balance: (Value Added *less* expenditure)	-92	14	-124	28	-348	-45	-650	55

Source: Urban and regional policy with provisional regional accounts, 1966–78, *Cambridge Economic Policy Review* (July 1980), Vol. 6, No. 2, based on Appendix, Provisional Regional Accounts. (Column totals may not be exact because of rounding errors.)

For 1978 personal disposable income per capita was 81 per cent. of the United Kingdom average; the next lowest region was Wales with 91 per cent.[2]

Value Added and Expenditure

It should come as no surprise in the light of the previous discussion that the volume of real goods and services produced per person in Northern Ireland or more formally output or value added per capita is much smaller than the average for the United Kingdom as a whole. Detailed figures are shown in Table 3. In 1966 value added per capita at factor cost, which is generally the preferred measure of output and where factor cost nets out the effects on market prices of subsidies and indirect taxes, was only 68 per cent. of the United Kingdom figure but by 1978 it had risen to some 75 per cent. of the latter. Government services made up 13 per cent. of value added per capita in 1966 but had risen to 21 per cent. by 1978; the comparable figures for the United Kingdom are 11 per cent. and 14 per cent. In fact the growing importance of government economic activity in the Northern Ireland economy is further substantiated by the data presented in Table 3.

For the years shown and indeed throughout the 1970s expenditure per capita has risen faster in Northern Ireland than in the rest of the United Kingdom and by 1978 was 97 per cent. of the average for the latter. One of the most striking features of the expenditure figures is the rise in public consumption expenditure relative to the United Kingdom as a whole. In 1966 and 1970 it was much the same in both areas but by 1978 it was 36 per cent. greater in Northern Ireland and represented 30 per cent. of total expenditure in comparison with 21 per cent. for the United Kingdom. It is true that some of this expenditure in Northern Ireland is a direct consequence of the " troubles " but it again emphasises the growing quantitative importance of the public sector.

It is difficult to assess the significance for the Northern Ireland economy of its increasing dependence on the public sector and more broadly public expenditure, which includes not only public consumption and investment expenditure but also expenditure transfers to the private sector. It is of fundamental importance to human welfare and the maintenance of economic activity and employment in the short term. By the same token the economy is extremely vulnerable to cuts in public expenditure. In the longer term it may

[2] Urban and regional policy with provisional regional accounts, 1966–78, *Cambridge Economic Policy Review* (July 1980), Vol. 6, No. 2, p. 33.

be that the extensive dependence on public expenditure and on a large public sector in which productivity improvements are difficult to achieve and where wages, salaries and conditions of work are determined by those operating in Great Britain, tends to raise wages and prices in the private sector with adverse effects on its output and employment.

Table 3 also shows a rapidly growing disparity in Northern Ireland between expenditure and value added per capita. The nominal figures clearly exaggerate the growth of the disparity in real terms, but in 1978 at £650 per capita representing a deficit between expenditure and value added of £1,001 million, it nevertheless indicates an enormous transfer of resources to Northern Ireland and, of necessity, is of profound economic, social and political significance.

Policy Approaches

The Northern Ireland Government, in attempting to stimulate economic development, has for many years offered assistance in the form of grants and cheap loans for capital investment on terms not matched in other parts of the United Kingdom. In addition to this it offers grants towards starting up costs which are based on the numbers employed, gives training grants, 75 per cent. industrial derating and financial support to what are considered to be firms in short-term difficulties.

Whilst this approach to development is flexible and gives discretionary powers to government the major emphasis remains subsidies of capital which, as is well known, raises difficult questions about its appropriateness when the surplus factor is labour. Moreover, despite the incentives to capital investment, industrial output has declined as a proportion of total output since the 1960s. In 1966 it was some 45 per cent. of value added, was 38 per cent. in 1970 and 37 per cent. in 1978; and it has already been indicated how employment has declined in the manufacturing sector. In these circumstances, and in no way wishing to diminish the difficulties in encouraging development during the troubles and violence of the 1970s, it is hard not to feel that the results have been disappointing. Before turning to an examination of different forms of subsidy, however, we should like to raise a quite separate policy issue, applicable at the national level, namely a negative income tax.

Negative Income Tax

Under this proposal, which has been advocated by leading economists of very different schools of thought, unemployment benefit is replaced by a payment (negative income tax) equal to a fraction (k) of the difference between earned income and a base-line income level (y_0). If earned income exceeds the base-line level, income tax is payable. The major advantage lies in the incentives to work which the scheme would create, since the earner's disposable income would rise with earnings. Under the present income maintenance scheme, there is a strong disincentive for the earner to work, at least overtly, unless his earnings would exceed unemployment benefit plus an amount dependent on the dis-utility of work.

Workers with low-income earning capacity, currently demanded by employers only at wage rates too low to be acceptable given the present benefit system, would find employment, would increase their disposable income given sensible choice of k and y_0 and employment in the economy would rise. The proportionate employment gains would probably be greatest in the weaker regions where the proportionate levels of unemployment are higher.

How the introduction of a negative income tax would affect trade union demands for wage rates for their members is unclear but would surely depend on the effect on the disposable income of a representative worker which would be little different for appropriate choice of k and y_0.

It is possible that untrammelled operation of a negative income tax would, of itself, go a long way towards generating full employment. Regional differences in wage rates would emerge more freely and workers with insufficient skills to find employment at current wage rates would have far greater chances of finding work. Governments in the past have shown reluctance to introduce this change in the tax system, so we consider below an alternative measure, a marginal wages subsidy.

Marginal Employment Subsidy

It must be borne in mind that prosperity in the Province is heavily dependent on prosperity in Great Britain. We advocate below a policy for Northern Ireland of subsidising job creation through a marginal wages subsidy, while recognising that this policy might be applied at the national level in current circumstances.[3] Nationally applied, a marginal employment subsidy might be sufficiently stimulating to

---

[3] If acceptable under the Treaty of Rome. Art. 92, s. 3, appears permissive for its application in depressed regions. It is true that the Commission has consistently opposed subsidies on operating costs and aids to declining industries, but the high unemployment levels in Europe of recent years have produced pressures too strong for the Commission to resist.

reduce the regional problem to an acceptable dimension. This is probably optimistic but in the present paper we assume that marginal employment subsidies will not be generally applied.

Some of the difficulties faced by the Northern Ireland economy are easy to discern. The currency is sterling so that there is no possible adjustment of the exchange rate to suit Northern Ireland— the Northern Ireland exchange rate is necessarily that rate which is determined on the exchanges for the United Kingdom economy as a whole. Isolated from her main markets by sea, Northern Ireland business faces transport costs in imports (an increasing burden with significantly rising energy costs), which push up manufacturing costs and consumer prices of imports and at the same time require that export prices be sufficiently low to compensate for transport costs in exports. Free movement of capital forces interest rates to equate to national rates, leaving no freedom for local monetary policy and, of course, Northern Ireland has no legal powers for autonomous fiscal action. It is our conviction that this situation makes the drive for wage parity with Britain a mistaken policy and that, in fact, real wages have a persistent tendency to be above the full employment level.

This is not to suggest that we advocate wage cuts, a policy which would probably be rendered impracticable by the trade union movement and which, if it were to lead to high employment, might require unacceptably low wages. An interesting quotation from J. M. Keynes illustrates the problem and provides, for us, the appropriate analysis: " If we decide that the interests of justice and charity require that the income of the working class should be higher than that which they receive from the economic machine, then we must, so to speak, subscribe to that end. Taxation is a measure of compulsory subscription, and the subscription must be spread over the whole community. But if that subscription is made to fall solely on a particular body of employers then we must not be surprised if the level of employment and output is below what it should be." [4]

The costs of employing labour include, in addition to wages, the costs of national insurance contributions and surcharges plus potentially significant redundancy payments, the latter relating to costs of firing and acting as a disincentive to recruitment. While these non-wages costs are not insignificant, the main costs arise through wages and a policy of wage subsidies naturally arises for consideration. We

---

[4] " The Question of High Wages ", THE POLITICAL QUARTERLY (Jan. 1930), p. 115.

are well aware of the inherent dangers of such a policy but believe this policy to be worth serious consideration in current circumstances.

In our opinion, economic analysis of wage subsidies, and indeed subsidies in general, is by no means fully developed. This is probably in large measure due to difficulties in tracing out secondary effects [5] of the subsidies without a complete model. Subsidies and taxes can readily be incorporated in neoclassical models but problems arise, first, in defining such models which are consistent with unemployment and, secondly and related, in incorporating money and absolute price levels in a satisfactory way. Pending the solution of these problems, the question of the efficacy of subsidies in a neoclassical world must be answered at a less rigorous level.

Consider some of the main arguments advanced against subsidising wages:

(1) The subsidy is a transfer of income from taxpayers to the subsidised industry, say industry X. Taxes come from consumers and other industries so that other industries are smaller in order to bolster industry X. A net loss arises as capital and labour are driven out of healthy industries to industry where they are less efficient so that less output is created in total.

(2) Most of the subsidies would accrue to workers already in employment and on whom there would accordingly be no savings in unemployment benefit. Thus the PSBR would increase with inflationary consequences.

(3) Subsidies on new employment would merely induce firms to expand their labour force rather than extend the average hours worked per week of existing labour employed.

(4) Since it is difficult to distinguish between industries in short-term recession induced decline and industries in long-term decline, subsidies would inhibit healthy structural change.

(5) It is difficult to time the cessation of subsidies appropriately and political pressure could lead to subsidies intended as a short-term measure becoming long-term support.

(6) Adoption of the policy would lead, as unemployment declined, to demands for higher wages which would not be strenuously opposed by employers in hopes of increased subsidies. There would accordingly be a continuous upward pressure on both wages and subsidies which would ultimately raise the burden of non-wage earners beyond the benefit.

---

[5] ". . . the direct economic effect of a tax or a bounty never constitutes the whole, and very often not even the chief part of the considerations which have to be weighed before deciding to adopt " (Marshall, *Principles of Economics*, Book V, XIII, 7).

These arguments are certainly to be taken seriously but are surely far from decisive in present circumstances. The first carries less weight, the greater the extent of unemployment. The gains in extra output come from employing unemployed resources which can be drawn not from other industry but from the dole queue. Relative costs need not markedly alter if the subsidy is applied as a marginal subsidy available to all firms as proposed by, say, Layard and Nickell.[6] Under this scheme, a subsidy is paid on *all new* jobs created in a firm. " If introduced in year t, the scheme could be guaranteed to last in this form until the end of year t + 2 and to go on being paid thereafter in relation to the average number of jobs in year t + 2 or the then current level, whichever is the less. However, the subsidy per worker would fall progressively to zero over, say, four years."

The second can be dismissed if the subsidy is a marginal one.

The third seems an advantage rather than a problem from a social point of view and carries no clear economic disadvantages.

The fourth does not arise if the marginal subsidy is payable in principle to all firms.

Five and six can be obviated by including the timing and duration in the introductory legislation. This would also hinder the formation of counter-productive expectations on the part of employers and employees and help keep wage claims in check. The danger of the gains being dissipated through high wages is a real one, however, although we have less fears of this with a marginal subsidy than a general subsidy which would have a much greater effect on average costs.

Given that subsidies are being paid in Northern Ireland, to date mainly on capital, we would suggest that it would be appropriate to substitute some of these for marginal labour subsidies, at least for a short period of years. The effects on unemployment would be confidently expected to be greater than with capital subsidies although the differential effects on output and growth of output are harder to estimate. The poor record of capital subsidisation adds weight to the suggestion which in fact has been made in reference to Northern Ireland on previous occasions. The 1962 Hall Report [7] discussed it in Sections 115–121 and 205–206 but the members of the Joint Working Party were unable to recommend it unanimously.

---

[6] Layard and Nickell, " The Case for Subsidising Extra Jobs ", *Economic Journal*, 90, 357 (March 1980), pp. 51–73.

[7] Report of the Joint Working Party on the Economy of Northern Ireland, Cmnd. 1835 (October 1962).

The more recent Quigley Report [8] also discussed it in Sections 16.13–16.14. They saw merit in it and felt that it should be largely self-financing, taking into account the gain in output and employment which implies increased taxes and a saving in unemployment benefit.

The efficacy of the subsidy applied in Northern Ireland would depend mainly on the elasticity of demand for labour and the effect on product prices. The more elastic is the former, the greater are the likely gains, given prices. The elasticity of demand for labour tends to be greater, the greater is the elasticity of demand for the final product. Northern Ireland as a small economy with a fixed exchange rate *vis-à-vis* its main market is essentially a price-taker and accordingly is faced by elastic demand for its products. With the fall in marginal cost induced by the subsidy, it could expect to sell considerable extra output without dampening prices, especially when account is taken of the extra demand generated in the Province itself. Accordingly, we would have considerable hopes of gains with a well-defined marginal employment subsidy and would urge that it be tried as soon as is practicable.

Social and Political Implications

Persistent heavy unemployment rates tend to have serious social effects in any advanced economy. In a society as divided politically and culturally as Northern Ireland, these effects are exacerbated. With considerable excess supply of labour at observed wage rates, opportunities are afforded for employers to discriminate on sectarian or other criteria in their hiring policies and, just as important, accusations of employer discrimination, whatever the realities, can gain plausibility. Considerable pressures are thereby placed on employers, but the fact that suspicion can and does arise, despite the efforts of such bodies as the Fair Employment Agency, is sufficient to accentuate the political and sectarian conflict. Whilst full employment or excess demand for labour would not solve Northern Ireland's political and cultural conflicts it can scarcely be doubted that it would ameliorate them and perhaps go some way to undermining feelings of alienation and antipathy towards the whole society. It might even do more in so far as the willingness to engage in or condone violence is facilitated by the lack of employment and the sense of social rejection which it encourages.

It is also evident that the scarcity of employment in the private sector, epitomised by the worrying rate of decline of employment in

[8] Economic and Industrial Strategy for Northern Ireland, Belfast HMSO (1976).

manufacturing industry, has helped to induce expansion of the public sector and made Northern Ireland relatively more dependent than any other region of the United Kingdom on public expenditure and on transfers from the central government on an enormous scale. This must be a matter of concern to British governments preoccupied with reducing government spending. The scale of the transfers is also fundamentally relevant to the political future of Northern Ireland and especially to those who advocate some form of united or federal Ireland or to those who in certain circumstances would contemplate a form of independence for the Province. There seems to be insufficient appreciation amongst the public at large or the public representatives of Northern Ireland of the extreme precariousness of the position of the Northern Ireland economy and the implications this has for its political future. New and imaginative economic measures are desperately needed and it is a matter of the utmost concern that there is little evidence any such measures are in the offing.

WAGE BARGAINING AND UNEMPLOYMENT

SEAN GLYNN AND STEPHEN SHAW

KEITH MIDDLEMAS, in his article in this journal last October, raises what seems certain to become the central issue of economic and political life during the 1980s, that is to say the impact of levels of unemployment which are unprecedented since the 1920s and 1930s. His conclusions are extremely pessimistic: the cost in economic dislocation and social unrest will far outweigh the putative benefits of reduced inflation, diminished union power, and an ultimately revitalised private sector. We strongly agree with this bleak prognosis. We will examine in greater detail the impact of unemployment upon the trade unions, particularly in the light of inter-war experience.

Some early indications of the response of organised labour to the Government's economic strategy and to the rapid increase in the level of unemployment are already visible. While the Conservative Party remains in office, the union movement is committed to a policy of free collective bargaining and opposition to legislation covering " secondary picketing ", ballots, and the closed shop. Equally, the Government's overall economic strategy has now emerged with some clarity. Growth and employment are being heavily sacrificed in order to combat inflation in a situation of deepening recession. In practice the policy is more accurately described as deflation rather than true and effective monetarism. The intention is to make the unions " see reality " by threatening them with a sharp increase in unemployment and job insecurity which is attributed (rightly or wrongly) to " excessive " wage demands and to stiffen employer resistance.

It has usually been accepted that, except in highly exceptional circumstances, wage settlements should at least match the rise in the cost of living over the preceding and/or the anticipated settlement period (usually the latter). The Social Contract was one example of such an exceptional period and it is clear that the Thatcher Government hopes to convince wage-bargainers that, in less happy

* Sean Glynn is Senior Lecturer, University of Kent, and joint author, with John Oxborrow, of *Interwar Britain: A Social and Economic History* (George Allen and Unwin, 1976). Stephen Shaw recently completed a doctoral thesis on inter-war unemployment and the trade union movement.

circumstances, they have entered another. Over the past decade, despite high inflation, wages have tended to rise faster than prices. However, gross wage increases which just match the cost-of-living increase will normally fail to maintain net real earnings. This is particularly the case with low-paid workers. Even full indexation (*ex post*) would fail to maintain real net incomes.

It is extremely difficult to bargain on net earnings in order to compensate for changes in the cost of living. In so far as this is a (frequently vague) objective, several complications arise because of imperfect (and *ex post*) indexation of income tax, national insurance contributions and welfare benefits. Of course, this is an oversimplification of actual wage negotiating situations where the aim to at least preserve real take-home pay is only one of many possible considerations. In particular, the desire to restore or maintain traditional differentials is frequently important. On the other side of the coin the wage base taken in negotiations may be viewed, at least by employers, as " unrealistic " in the light of ensuing wage-payment patterns. Bonus schemes, allowances, increments and general wage drift invariably complicate and distort the picture. The fact remains that simple comparisons between (gross) wage settlements and official measures of inflation can be misleading and will not accurately reflect changes in real incomes. In general, wages must rise faster than prices in order to maintain living standards. Under existing Government policies wage negotiators will be pressed to accept substantial cuts in real incomes and to trade wages against jobs. How are they likely to respond? Are the behavioural assumptions about trade-union reactions valid? While the policy faces other political constraints (particularly, high interest rates), its ultimate feasibility rests upon influencing wage bargaining through the level of unemployment. What predictions may be made about wage negotiations in situations where unions are asked to accept cuts in real income and to trade wages against jobs?

Wages versus Jobs

Faced with the threat of redundancies, which may or may not be attributable to wage costs, will negotiators be willing to trade wages against work? In the small firm this situation may be seen in stark reality if the employer can convince workers that a particular wage increase will inevitably result in substantial redundancies or bankruptcy and closure. Firms in financial difficulties will, in effect, be asking their workers to subsidise them by accepting cuts in real wages—with the threat of unemployment if they refuse. There have already been many examples. This situation can also occur in large firms, such as British Leyland, and in the public sector where low-paid hospital and local authority staff may be asked to finance public spending cuts by accepting a lower standard of living. However, most wage negotiators will not be confronted with the threat of unemployment in such immediate terms. Even with unemployment in excess of 2 million the vast majority will remain in more or less secure employment. Equally, while long-term unemployment has increased, it remains a minority of the unemployed. Unions in a stronger bargaining position may not be impressed by arguments that in seeking to maintain their members' real income they are threatening the employment of others. Indeed, they may argue that a cut in their purchasing power could cause even more unemployment. Finally, it is open to them to argue that the national unemployment problem is a matter for governments rather than the direct concern of individual trade unions, which exist to protect the interests of their members. In other words, the Government has established the rules, but the unions may refuse to play the game.

Even in the public sector, whether unions are "militant" or not, it is by no means certain that earnings will be traded against employment, despite spending cuts, economies, cash limits and other employment-restricting measures. In so far as the threat of unemployment does succeed in restraining wage demands, there will be wide differentials in wage settlements under free collective bargaining. Powerful groups in efficient, profitable industries will succeed in obtaining relatively generous settlements which will raise costs (and prices) despite the likely increase in productivity bargaining to absorb costs. On the other hand, inefficient and less profitable industries will tend to obtain relatively cheap labour. Social justice aside, this may not be a sound prescription for a more efficient economy, nor a means of promoting a desirable re-structuring of industry and employment. It will reinforce, not break, the cycle of relatively low pay and low productivity which characterises much of British industry.

Opinions on trade unions reactions to unemployment have changed greatly in the past two decades. It is not clear whether trade union and electoral sensitivity to unemployment was exaggerated (for example, by approaches based on "Phillips Curve" analysis and related concepts); but there is evidence to suggest that tolerance of unemployment has increased and the actual level of unemployment which is consistent with political success is now higher than was previously supposed.[1] In the 1979 General Election the fact that 1·5 million people were jobless received much less attention than it might have done in the 1960s. At the same time, it remains apparent that unemployment is a highly sensitive political issue and this has influenced more recent government attitudes. For example, the reversal in policies of the Heath Government was related to concern about increasing unemployment; and the specific timing of the reversal was, according to some sources, related to the threat of violence if redundancies were created on Clydeside. Even the most committed monetarists are aware of the political dangers and economic and social costs of raising unemployment. The fear that unemployment may be associated with electoral failure is added to further fears about the breakdown of State authority and the rise of extremist political groupings. In addition, it is held that unemployment among young people increases the likelihood of individualised acts of delinquency and that unemployment among ethnic minorities increases the chances of a rapid deterioration in community relations.

On the other hand, the " full employment " experienced in the 1950s and early 1960s is clearly over, and this seems to have gained a fair degree of political and academic acceptance. There is also a growing awareness that certain secular trends within the economy indicate that increased levels of unemployment are likely in the future. Micro-technology has received a good deal of attention in terms of the shedding of labour, but it is not the only factor. Also exerting an influence are changing patterns in work preferences and retirement provisions, changes in unemployment benefits and redundancy payments, as well as low growth rates and direct market influences affecting workforce structure. By post-war standards, unemployment has remained high throughout the 1970s and seems likely on the basis of existing trends to increase rather than diminish in both the short and medium term. While the tolerance level has been lifted, few doubt that some kind of political flashpoint remains. However, if the Government's " short, sharp shock " is to succeed it must surely involve a level of unemployment comparable with the 1930s, and far in excess of anything experienced in the period since 1945. The expression " highest since the war " has now given way to just these comparisons with the inter-war period. But apart from the question of the necessary magnitude of unemployment which monetarists believe will make unions " see reality ", there is also the

---

[1] For example, in Peter Jay's pamphlet, *A General Hypothesis of Employment, Inflation and Politics* (I.E.A., 1976).

question of duration. A " short, sharp shock " may, like incomes policies, prove to be effective only for a very limited period.

Trade Union Reaction

Although the trade union movement has begun to give some attention to the unemployment problem, the nature of their reactions is blurred by linking unemployment with the quite separate question of a shorter working week. This latter demand is likely to be a major feature of the 1980s, not only in Britain, and an important part of the response to secular trends in unemployment. For example, the Transport and General Workers Union has said:

"With more than $1\frac{1}{4}$ million people out of work in this country, the TGWU, Britain's strongest union, believes that urgent action is necessary to turn the tide of unemployment.

We propose that the Labour movement makes the thirty-five hour week, with no loss of pay, a top priority in the fight to bring down the number of workers unemployed.

We believe that the thirty-five hour week will create 750,000 new jobs.

We do not say that it will be easy, but that it is the only way forward and that free collective bargaining will be vitally important to bring it about." [2]

Of course, this does not represent any willingness to trade wages against employment, and the argument behind the belief (based on Trade Union Research Unit calculations) that the 35-hour week could create 750,000 new jobs is not wholly convincing. On the contrary, it seems possible that in current circumstances such a huge increase in unit costs could actually eliminate jobs on a substantial scale. The detailed calculations depend on heroic assumptions about overtime and productivity. However, to the embarrassment of the parliamentary leadership, the claim for a 35-hour week without loss of pay has been adopted as the policy of the Labour Party and as an integral part of the TUC's alternative economic strategy. The conclusion of the 1979 Engineering dispute will add a substantial impetus to the demand for reduced hours.

The varying employment prospects in different industries, and the constitutional limits upon TUC powers, suggest that several *ad hoc* union strategies will emerge. In general, unions will seek to preserve jobs as in the past, but they will strenuously resist doing so at the expense of real wages or wage rates. The TUC will increasingly seek to make it clear that unemployment is a national Government responsibility, and will continue to reject the argument that real wage reductions can increase employment, on the grounds

[2] *Tribune* (September 7, 1979).

that they further reduce domestic demand. In export industries the exchange rate is a greater problem than potential wage rises (it also intensifies import competition). The Government appears to view the exchange rate either as a " given " (*i.e.* beyond its control) and/ or as an anti-inflation device. Any improvement in export competitiveness might therefore be nullified by a stronger balance of payments and a dearer rate for sterling. In many industries, for example textiles, price competitiveness could only be restored by unacceptable cuts in real wages. Particular unions are likely to continue to press for import controls and employment subsidies. The traditional recourse to short-time working has already proved to be part of the strategy in many industries. Short time is usually regarded as a temporary expedient, although in present circumstances it may become both more extensive and more durable.

Unions and the Unemployed

For the trade unions the struggle against unemployment is essentially a political struggle. The use of industrial action against unemployment is considered to be almost foredoomed to failure. Trade union powers are very limited and unemployment must be tackled nationally. Since the late 1960s, governments have tended to use unemployment as a tool of economic management and this has greatly intensified under the present administration. Ostensibly at least, the Government has tended to ignore the TUC and is in no mood for compromise. Deals like the Social Contract of the 1970s or the recent Australian agreement between the Australian Congress of Trade Unions and the Australian Labour Party, or co-operation as in West Germany have been ruled out. Unions have been left to deal with the situation in an *ad hoc* manner as best they can. The alternatives are toothless political protest or to resort to the streets, which would be anathema to the present TUC leadership.

Is it inevitable then that a split will emerge between the employed and the unemployed? The experience during the 1920s and 1930s provides the best available evidence of how trade unionists react to a continuing high level of unemployment. While unemployment was genuinely abhorred, the links between trade unionists and the unemployed were weak in the localities and virtually non-existent at the centre. While in some industries—coal-mining and elements of the textile trades—relations between employed and unemployed were much closer, there was still room for antagonism and in South Wales the system of miners' lodges was re-organised as the unemployed came to dominate policy-making.

In other words, organisationally the employed were separated from the unemployed. However, unemployment is a moving stream —one of the factors which makes more difficult any organisation of the jobless—and the split was only really with the long-term unemployed who represented only a minority of the total. Moreover, the unemployed—then as now—contain many non-unionists, women, and young workers, so the gap between the unions and the unemployed is not simply a function of unemployment itself. The "marginalisation" of the unemployed between the wars was the result of a number of different calculations on the part of the TUC including distaste for the non-unionist, recognition of individual union autonomy, and anti-Communism, as well as the lack of an immediate economic motive for organising the unemployed. It is important, therefore, not to exaggerate the gap between employed and unemployed. Certain groups and particular regions are highly vulnerable. The TUC has pressed for measures to help them. Long-term unemployment covers only a small minority of the total and job turnover is fairly high. For this reason alone, concern about unemployment is more widespread than the unemployment total itself might suggest. Job insecurity is widespread. The division between the employed and the unemployed is not finite but is constantly changing.

One of the mechanisms for transmitting the fear of unemployment into modified wage demands is a decline in union membership. There is evidence that this decline is now occurring, much to union disquiet. Certainly, as with any organisation, a decline in membership imposes a financial constraint upon activities. However, as will be shown below, union membership declined dramatically during the 1920s and 1930s but without a consequential impact on wages. So long as the percentage unionised in areas of collective agreements does not fall, the impact of membership loss on union power is minimal. At the 1980 TUC there was some discussion of organising the unemployed although presently many unions make little effort to retain as members workers who are made redundant. The "Right to Work" marches organised by the Socialist Workers' Party have been shunned—a mirror image of the attitude to the Hunger Marches 50 years earlier—and the Claimants' Union has been kept at arm's length by the TUC. Perhaps more surprisingly, trade unionists have virtually ignored the real cuts in social security benefits announced for 1980 and 1981, and the abandonment of earnings-related supplement in 1982. This is quite unlike the 1930s and presumably suggests some lack of concern for the standards of the jobless, as well as a belief that these cuts will not influence wage bargaining.

The growth in unemployment has outstripped all but the most pessimistic forecasts. Perhaps for this reason our impression is that the unions are taking a closer interest in the unemployed than was the case for most of the inter-war period. However, formal links—particularly with the young—would be difficult to forge no matter what the intentions of the TUC. But our feeling is that the danger of a split between the employed and unemployed is essentially a result of the growth of the hard-core long-term unemployed rather than the outlook of the trade unions themselves.

A Comparison

It is difficult to find any close contemporary comparisons for the type of situation which British society now faces. Although there are approximate parallels in other economies, the British situation is probably, to a degree, *sui generis*. Nevertheless, in purely British terms it is possible, as Middlemas has shown, to make what may be a very significant comparison with the inter-war years when the trade union movement faced a 20-year period of large-scale redundancy, with unemployment continually in excess of 10 per cent. of the (insured) workforce. At times, in the early 1920s and 1930s, the level exceeded 20 per cent. and the overall average was about 14 per cent., representing around 1·5 million workers. Ostensibly, the inter-war years were different from the present in that the economy tended to experience deflation rather than inflation. Yet fear of inflation was an important factor prompting government policy and it was widely accepted that " excessive wages " were the basic cause of contemporary economic difficulties including unemployment and the poor performance of the export industries. Wage " flexibility ", in other words a drop in (money) wages, was regarded as the root solution in official and academic circles. Keynes was one of the few important dissentients from this analysis. He accepted that wages were not flexible downwards and set out to devise alternative policies. Eventually he arrived at what was regarded as a " revolution " in economic theory.

The period was a difficult one for the trade union movement—which was weaker in terms of membership and influence than it is today. Trade union membership declined so that at its lowest in 1933 it was at level barely half that of its peak only 13 years earlier. While a substantial improvement was made in the remainder of the 1930s, the 1920 peak was not regained before the outbreak of the

Second World War. Unions could claim to cover only a minority of wage-earners and the movement had apparently sustained a major defeat in the General Strike of 1926. Yet, after the reductions imposed in 1921 and 1922, the union movement struggled successfully to enforce a high degree of rigidity upon wages. Even when the substantial gains which had been won in the brief, militant aftermath of the 1914–18 War were under attack in the slump of the early 1920s, unions successfully protected their reduced hours of work. In general, after 1922 money wages were held and, in a situation of falling prices, this implied a substantial improvement in *real* standards for the vast majority who remained in employment. Between 1923 and 1937 average weekly earnings remained constant while retail prices fell by about 15 per cent. The General Strike may be seen as a test case on the wages issue, and while the strike has been commonly regarded as a defeat for the union movement and a disaster for the miners, it had demonstrated the strength of worker solidarity. In 1925, Baldwin is alleged to have told the miners that all workers faced a reduction in wages, and this had been implicit in Government policy since the beginning of the decade. The actual experience of the General Strike left no desire among employers or Government for a repetition and, with the sad exception of the miners, the wages front tended to hold. During the downturn in the economy after 1929, the pressure for reductions in wages was intensified. But the reductions effected, while quite extensive, were not substantial and did not prevent a continuing general improvement in real standards. Some groups of workers—such as the Engineers—escaped reductions almost entirely. On the other hand, there were general cuts in public sector wages. Naval pay cuts provoked the " Invergordon mutiny " which finally forced Britain off the Gold Standard. Most public sector employees, however, were not unionised.

The official trade union attitude during the inter-war period was that wages were to be held at all costs, and attempts to impose reductions were to be strenuously resisted. This attitude was exhibited and expressed most openly in the mining industry in the mid-1920s. For example, in the negotiations before the General Strike the Government intervened to press the case for wage reductions in coal-mining:

" Baldwin pointed out that without the subsidy many mines would have to close unless wages were cut; on the December quarter's figures almost all the pits in Northumberland would close, 97 per cent. in Durham, 90 per cent. in South Wales, etc. Would the miners be prepared for unemployment for perhaps 200,000 of their members? Smith replied that the creation of some unemployment would be a lesser evil than a reduction in the living standards of all miners." [3]

Another miners' leader, Tom Richards, had remarked: "We are concerned not so much as to how many men are employed, but how they live when they are employed in this industry", and union leaders in general argued that unemployment was a governmental and not a trade union responsibility. The primary objective of trade union action was the protection of wages. It was argued that wage reductions (that is, the equivalent of wage restraint in present circumstances) were emphatically not an employment-creating policy. On the contrary, unions argued that wage reductions inevitably reduced purchasing power and consumer spending, resulting in more unemployment. This view owed more to Hobson's underconsumptionist theory than to Keynes, although Bevin—perhaps alone among trade union leaders—does appear to have understood the basis of the Keynesian argument.

While the trade union leaders remained entirely committed to their first principle of holding wages at almost any cost, they were concerned, however, with a general range of measures to relieve unemployment; and they took some part in organised protests against the lack of effective government action. There was no consistent trade union unemployment policy, but among the measures which were advocated were increased public works spending (although this was seen only as a palliative), trade promotion (notably with the Soviet Union, and for a brief period, with the Empire), raising the school-leaving age, encouraging emigration and retirement, and restricting overtime. There are contemporary echoes here. The inter-war union movement also exhibited a healthy, if over-optimistic, interest in rationalisation where this seemed likely to promote industrial efficiency and not simply cartelisation, reduced capacity, and redundancies. As faith in rationalisation diminished during the downturn of the early 1930s, the improvements in efficiency which had been effected were used to bolster the general demand for reduced hours and work-sharing. There is perhaps an analogy between this attitude and the contemporary union response to the "New Technology". Reductions in hours were of course not to be accompanied by wage reductions. However, in relation to both short-time and overtime there was some official acceptance of reduced earnings (but not of wage rates), although this was highly unpopular with union rank and file.

[3] Margaret Morris, *The General Strike* (Penguin, 1976), p. 202.

Above all, the policy of holding wages remained, and it achieved a considerable degree of success in the face of very adverse industrial, economic and political circumstances. The obvious question is how were the inter-war unions able to succeed with this policy in what seems to have been a very unfavourable climate for wages? The answer rests in the unions' own strength which, despite some diminution, was retained at a sufficient level to prevent employers and governments enjoying any marked success in forcing wages downwards. The solidarity demonstrated during the General Strike might have escalated the conflict into a genuine constitutional and political issue if it had continued for weeks rather than days (which was precisely what frightened the TUC leaders themselves).

So how was union strength maintained in such adverse circumstances? First, not all unions were equally affected by unemployment, and unionisation remained high in certain industries and firms. The newly established system of national bargaining in most industries reduced flexibility. It is possible, too, that traditional union loyalties, together with the influence of the Unemployed Movement (led by Communists) may have done something to prevent strike-breaking and the undercutting of union agreements.[4] But ultimately, the strength of the trade unions and of unorganised workers also rested upon the social security system. This was a mixture of National Insurance, what became known as the " Dole " under a series of official titles, and the remnants of the 19th Century Poor Law. The existence of this system both strengthened union resolve to resist demands for reductions, even at the cost of unemployment, and diminished the likelihood of an individual taking a position at less than the negotiated trade union rate. In effect, the " Dole " provided a national minimum standard. If not generous in its provision, it was sufficiently high to protect wages. Although there did exist a gap between welfare provision and prospective wages for most of the unemployed, it might be considered that the " poverty trap " has a long history. The " Dole " had been introduced almost by accident and as a supposedly temporary measure during the post-First World War boom, but it perhaps remained as the price of social stability.[5] The crisis which resulted when some benefits were cut by the introduction of new national scales in 1935 gave an illustration of the potential for social and political unrest which existed below the surface and which the " Dole " helped to contain. Without it,

---

[4] Sidney Pollard, "Trade Union Reactions to the Economic Crisis ", *Journal of Contemporary History* (1969), p. 114.
[5] Bentley B. Gilbert, *British Social Policy 1914–1939* (Batsford, 1970).

millions would have faced starvation and mass unemployment might have had a very different effect, however "marginalised" the grievances, and would have been viewed in a very different manner by the trade unions. As it was, they were able to leave the formal organisation of the unemployed mainly to Communists, although along with the middle-class taxpayer, they continued to take a close interest in the social security system. In 1931 the TUC clashed with and broke the Labour Government on the issue of cutting the "Dole". The inter-war debate on unemployment benefits was conducted largely in terms of their cost and their impact upon the desire to work and upon wage rates. Current debate is returning to these issues.

Conclusions

Of course history may not tell us anything. But if the record of the inter-war period gives any indications they are that the "short, sharp shock" strategy can have at best only limited success in the British context unless it is very powerfully reinforced by much more savage cuts in public spending, drastic changes in social security provisions, and a willingness to combat serious social disorders. In other words, a price in terms of political unpopularity which no democratic government could conceivably contemplate for more than a very brief period. Equally severe will be the cost in economic disruption. Nor can there be any guarantee that any impact upon wage bargaining—so expensively obtained—will be anything but temporary. The results of the policies followed by inter-war governments, whatever else may be claimed for them, are not a happy precedent for Mrs. Thatcher's economic strategy.

WALES: WILL UNEMPLOYMENT BREED UNREST OR APATHY?

JOHN OSMOND

" We are impressed by the conviction of some of our witnesses who stress the risks of serious social disorder if there were to be very high and chronic levels of unemployment, particularly among the young. Wales, if condemned to suffer the incidence of workless-ness endured in the Thirties, is unlikely to respond with the apathy and despair that enveloped so many in those days: nor in any event, would it be tolerable to risk the economic and social collapse of local communities. When such real risks abound, it is imperative that the politics of prevention be practised."

—*First Report of the Committee on Welsh Affairs*, para. 28;
July 31, 1980.

THIS remarkable paragraph from the first report of Leo Abse's Select Committee on Welsh Affairs was designed to catch the head-lines and it succeeded. *The Times* led with the story which, naturally, received very wide coverage in Wales itself. The inclusion of the paragraph was remarkable mainly because all 11 members of the Committee presumably approved it—they certainly signed the report—and a majority of them were Conservatives: six, to Labour's four and one Liberal. The report also contained a whole series of recommendations involving large increases in public expen-diture which, taken together, implied a major shift in the Govern-ment's central economic strategy.

In particular the Committee called for more funds for the Welsh Development Agency's factory-building programme; a selective temporary employment subsidy for employers in short-term diffi-culties; the criteria for regional selective assistance to be relaxed; the exemption limit for industrial development certificates to be reduced; new settling-in grants for employees moving into special develop-ment areas; an upgrading of the development area status of much of Wales; and generally more money for the Welsh Development Agency to avoid it having to concentrate most of its resources on the steel closure areas.

The main attention, however, given to the report focused on its dramatic predictions of the political and social consequences of

---

* The author, formerly a political correspondent of the *Western Mail*, is Editor of *ARCADE—Wales Fortnightly*, a new current affairs and cultural magazine and has written *Creative Conflict: The Politics of Welsh Devolution* (Routledge and Kegan Paul, 1978).

unemployment. Would social unrest materialise? And, indeed, was it necessary for this to happen before any fundamental attention would be paid to Welsh problems? As the *Western Mail* put it on the day following the appearance of the report: " Will the Government listen to the Select Committee? If it does not it will only have itself to blame if the social disorder forecast by the committee in such sombre terms materialises."

The report was published on the eve of the parliamentary recess and this was used by the Government as a convenient means of pushing it to one side. Privately the Secretary of State for Wales, Nicholas Edwards, stated he believed the recommendations of the report had been pitched too high. Inside the Welsh Office preparations of any reaction were suspended until a firmer indication of the future of the slimmed-down Port Talbot and Llanwern steel plants became available. It was well known, for instance, that the BSC was contemplating a further cutback in its steelmaking capacity from 15 million tonnes to 12 million tonnes or even as low as to 8 million tonnes. Since Llanwern and Port Talbot were already working to half their capacity one or both would be bound to be axed if there was any further contraction. And, if this happened, the side effects would be enormous. For example, Philip Weekes, the NCB's South Wales director, told the Select Committee that the loss of Llanwern coking coal sales would require the closure of 12 collieries (the South Wales coalfield is heading for a loss of more than £90m. in the 1980–81 financial year in any event).

Forecasts of Social Unrest

Nevertheless, forecasts of " social unrest "—never defined beyond the phrase—were initially greeted with a good deal of scepticism. After all, unemployment had been rising sharply for some time, the Welsh steel industry had undergone a massive contraction already, and reaction had been extraordinarily muted. A variety of factors were held responsible: the blow was cushioned by the generous golden handshakes and the make-up pay coming from EEC given to redundant steelworkers, while the dole for school-leavers represented more than they had been getting at school and many found work on temporary employment schemes. Some commentators referred to the inherent passivity of British society. As Eric Willis, an economist at the Polytechnic of Wales who has made a special study of Mid-Glamorgan's economic problems, put it:

It is important to remember that the intense depression of the 1930s led to nothing more violent than a series of marches and relatively peaceful demonstrations in Wales and the rest of the U.K. Similar conditions in Europe at the same time contributed significantly to the rise of fascism in Germany, Italy and Spain; Stalinism in Russia and near anarchy in France.

The passiveness of British society in the face of intense economic problems has been pinpointed by John Galbraith. He suggests that Britain is the only democratic country where the harsh monetarist policies theorised by Milton Friedman, and largely adopted by the present Government, could be given a thorough test without severe social unrest.

Comparing the 1980s with the 1930s is, of course, fraught with pitfalls. Leo Abse himself, speaking at a Welsh local authority convened conference on unemployment last October, referred to the 1930s and noted that times had changed. In particular, he drew attention to the role of women in society which had undergone a revolution. In the economic upheaval that was Wales in the 1930s, with more than 400,000 leaving the country to find work, he said women had acted as a great restraining and stabilising influence on their menfolk. But in the 1980s this safety valve was no longer present. Women themselves were now in the employment market, likely to react to redundancy in a similar way to men, and were more often than not to be found taking leading parts in industrial strife. Young people, too, Abse noted, had been brought up with much higher expectations than their counterparts in the 1930s. At the conference, held in Cardiff, there was general acceptance that the Government could not be deflected from its economic policies except by confrontation. As the Rev. Bob Morgan, from Merthyr, put it: " We are continually describing the problem, but it is a cure we require. Unless we inject some conflict into the situation we will get nowhere." And Graham Harries, of Ogwr council, said: " If Mrs. Thatcher is not for turning on her economic policies, she must take the consequences. If we mean business, it must come to a general strike. It will come to that unless there is a response to our demands."

It is unlikely, however, that such a traditional weapon as a strike —even a widespread one—will be deployed in defence of jobs in Wales. More likely will be a deliberate mobilisation of " social unrest " to deal with specific local circumstances leading to confrontations with the police and, thereby, with the Government. It was interesting that early last September such a course was already being seriously contemplated at the highest level in the Wales TUC and had been the subject of discussions between Wales TUC representatives and the British TUC in London. The Wales TUC had in mind the threatened closure of Llanwern steelworks which was seen as intolerable and the point where active resistance should be mounted. According to the minutes of a meeting held in London between the Wales TUC and the British TUC on September 19, the Wales TUC's general secretary said: "Any further job losses in Wales have to be seen against the background of an unemployment level averaging 11·5 per cent. The Welsh Nationalists have shown that the Government can be successfully challenged. What the TUC and the Wales TUC have to do is to mount a successful fight." The alternative to an organised trade union campaign, Wright warned, was that: "the Welsh themselves might take matters into their own hands, with all the social disorder that such a course of action would bring". These minutes were "leaked" to Y Faner Goch ("The Red Flag") the paper of the Welsh Socialist Republican Movement (a breakaway movement from Plaid Cymru, the Welsh Nationalist Party). The Welsh nationalist success referred to was, of course, the campaign, led by the Plaid Cymru president, to force the Government to honour its election pledge to establish the new Fourth television channel in Wales for Welsh language broadcasting. In mid-September the Government yielded to Gwynfor Evans's threatened hunger-strike over the issue. And at the following meeting of the Wales TUC general council in October, George Wright issued a statement that they would mount a campaign of "civil disobedience" in the event of Llanwern being closed. For him to have made that announcement he must have had the tacit support of the TUC in London which, according to another delegation, this time from Plaid Cymru, was looking to Wales to confirm its warnings that current economic policies would trigger social unrest.

The Worst Unemployment

All this was taking place against a background in which, in the regional unemployment table, Wales was moving into the worst position outside Northern Ireland. By September last year Wales' jobless total had risen to 129,114, a rate of 11·9 per cent., compared with 85,916 a year before. Table 1 shows that the relative position of Wales regarding unemployment in the United Kingdom regions has worsened markedly since 1974. Wales now has unemployment rates higher than the North and the rate of acceleration in 1979–80 suggests that it could equal Northern Ireland in a year or two.

Wales, of course, has been badly hit by the rundown of the steel industry. But despite this the main cause of steeply rising redundancies during 1980 was the recession. Last September the London Business School forecast that unemployment in Britain would rise

TABLE 1

Unemployed by Region

(Seasonally adjusted %)

Employment Region	1974 (Aug.)	1979 (Sept.)	1980 (Sept.)	% Increase 1974/80
Scotland	4.3	7.4	9.7	31
North	5.6	7.8	10.2	31
N. Ireland	6.9	10.5	13.3	27
N. West	4.0	6.5	9.2	42
Wales	4.5	7.1	10.3	45
S. West	2.7	5.4	6.8	26
Yorks & Humberside	3.1	5.7	7.6	49
W. Midlands	2.6	5.0	8.0	60
E. Midlands	2.4	4.2	6.6	57
E. Anglia	2.0	4.0	5.8	45
S. East	3.1	3.4	4.9	44

Source: Welsh Counties Committee and Council for the Principality (Welsh Districts), *Unemployment in Wales* (October 1980).

to 2¼ million by the Spring of 1981, and to an average of 2¾ million over the financial year 1981–82. In view of the School's monetarist outlook this forecast should not be viewed as especially alarmist. If it turns out to be correct, and assuming Wales's share of unemployment remains roughly the same as in the recent past— that is, roughly around 6½ per cent. of the British total—then we can expect unemployment in Wales by 1981–82 to average around 180,000. This is higher than all the forecasts made to the Welsh Select Committee during its hearings in early 1980. The highest estimate, 170,000 by 1983, made by the Department of Economics at University College, North Wales, was dismissed by Government spokesmen as being well beyond the pale. But if the Government were to close down either or both Llanwern and Port Talbot, it is certain that Wales's share of total unemployment would rise significantly about 6½ per cent., with the unemployment level pushing, in all probability, beyond 200,000.

Such frightening unemployment forecasts for Wales arise from its economic structure. At the turn of the century the coalfields of North and South Wales fuelled industrialisation. Later, major steel-making plants were established at Shotton, Cardiff, Port Talbot, Ebbw Vale and Newport. Downstream activities, such as steel finishing at Shotton and tinplate manufacture in South Wales, evolved to bring periods of relative prosperity to certain areas. But today the alarming slump in demand for steel is creating fears that this former crucible of industrialisation will be broken for many generations.

Welsh steel and coal are not the only important industries affected by technological change. In North West Wales the impact of the collapse of the slate-quarrying industry a quarter of a century ago was marked by a succession of large, labour-intensive projects which provided temporary employment. The most recent is the Dinorwig Hydro-Electric Pump Storage scheme. But as this comes to an end a workforce of more than 2,400 will be declared redundant over the next two to three years. These and other job losses will result in unemployment in Gwynedd rising to 11,600 (over 15 per cent.) by 1982, even after allowing for new jobs in the pipeline. Another major industry in North Wales which has suffered a fundamental decline is textiles, with a decrease of 3,500 jobs since 1970. Throughout Wales there has been, too, a reliance upon agriculture which since 1965 has lost 17,000 jobs, mainly because of more intensive methods of production. Table 2 compares employment in key Welsh industrial sectors with Great Britain. The disproportionate dependence on metal manufacture is clear. Similarly, the agricultural sector is more prominent in Wales than Britain as a whole:

TABLE 2

Employees in Employment, Selected Industries 1978

	Wales %	Great Britain %
Agriculture, forestry and fisheries	2·5	1·7
Mining and quarrying	3·9	1·5
Metal manufacture	7·0	2·1
Service industries	55·0	57·9

Source: *Department of Employment Gazette.*

In contrast, the growth industries of recent years, practically all in the service sector, are under-represented in Wales. An examination of job losses between 1965 and 1979 is very revealing. Employment in mining and quarrying fell by 60 per cent., in metal manufacture by 30 per cent. and in agriculture by 43 per cent. The number of jobs involved was substantial: 55,000 in mining and quarrying 30,000 in metal manufacture, and 17,000 in agriculture. The decline in these three sectors will inevitably continue, while the recession for as long as it lasts, will hit industry in other parts of the economy

WALES: WILL UNEMPLOYMENT BREED UNREST OR APATHY?

From January to August 1980, 44,000 redundancies were declared in Wales (20,000 in the steel industry)—an increase of 175 per cent. (28,000) on the previous year. As a region's basic industries disappear, the secondary and induced effects of major closures can decimate local manufacturing and service companies. At the same time the supply of labour over the next 10 years will increase: with 40,000 young people leaving school and the continuing trend for women to go out to work, the labour force in Wales is predicted to increase by a rate of nearly three times the national average.

Likely Responses

So even without the current recession and a Government bent on policies that give—at the time of writing—greater priority to the money supply and inflation than unemployment, Wales would face enormous problems of structural decline and imbalance in her economy. Given the ongoing attack on the less prosperous areas of the country by the present Government, what will the likely response in Wales actually be?

To tackle her problems Wales needs at least three responses:

(1) Massive new government investment in her infrastructure and, directly, in industry. It has to be government investment because there is no chance of enough coming from anywhere else, despite the fact that in the past decade there has been a significant increase in investment in Wales from overseas— notably from Japan and the United States.

(2) Determined economic planning to ensure that what investment does occur takes place in the context of a coherent long-term strategy; together with imaginative policies to encourage industrial development, such as the tax concessions that have been deployed in the Irish Republic.

(3) The development within Wales of a greater entrepreneurial spirit coupled with increased efforts to establish small co-operative ventures.

The Wales TUC is currently exploring the possibility of establishing a large Welsh co-operative enterprise along the lines of the successful Basque Mondragon co-operative in northern Spain. This entails workers investing a proportion of their savings or earnings, a worker-controlled bank and co-operative marketing consortiums and distribution outlets. For such an enterprise to get off the ground in Wales, it would probably require initial government assistance.

Just to list requirements such as these, in the present economic climate and with the present Government, merely highlights the difficulty. Positive responses along these lines are only likely to arise out of resistance on the ground to the central economic policies being pursued by the Government with their devastating effects on specific communities. And whether effective resistance can be mobilised in Wales remains, at the beginning of the 1980s, both the central and the most doubtful question in Welsh politics. Certainly the character of the Labour Party in Wales does not suggest that any especially radical leadership will be forthcoming from that quarter. Only five of the 23 Welsh Labour M.P.s supported a candidate of the Left or Centre in the recent Labour parliamentary leadership election and a majority of the constituency parties backed Denis Healey. Equally most local authorities in Wales, including those which are Labour-controlled, have been generally compliant in making the spending cuts demanded of them by central government.

This leaves the trade unions in Wales and Plaid Cymru as the only organisations consciously seeking a way, indeed a strategy, for confronting the present Government head on over the unemployment question. Probably unemployment will have to get much worse, with some further closures of steel mills and coal mines, before any real mobilisation will occur. There is potential for a campaign of disruption and direct politics on the unemployment issue in Wales. If such a campaign developed, it would mark a most significant change in the direction of Welsh politics. It is a change that any government in Westminster, whether Conservative or Labour-controlled, would have no interest in seeking. And probably for that reason alone ways will be found of preventing it happening. Certainly, any London government would be wise to seek ways of heading off an alliance between socialism and nationalism in Wales.

ADDENDUM

Last December the Government dismissed the large majority of the Welsh Select Committee's recommendations on rising unemployment in Wales and rejected its warning of " serious social disorder " as irresponsible. It could discourage inward investment and " act as a spur to a tiny minority interested in creating social disorder ", the Government said (Cmnd. 8085, para. 6). The response of the Committee's chairman, Leo Abse, was that his report's rejection would force the Welsh Labour movement to seek alternatives to constitutional action. At the time of writing the future of the Llanwern and Port Talbot steelworks remained uncertain.

UNEMPLOYMENT: THE PAST AND FUTURE OF A POLITICAL PROBLEM

KEITH MIDDLEMAS

RECENT weeks have witnessed a sudden, almost dramatic, concern with the growing total of unemployed in Britain, directed in particular to evidence of accelerated decline in certain towns and regions and unemployment among the young and ethnic minorities. During July, newspapers which had previously been favourably disposed to the government became more sharply critical (witness the *Sunday Times*, July 13). Coming after months in which conventional press wisdom maintained that the unemployed did not present a political threat—embodied in leaders with headlines such as " the absence of blood in the streets "—this must, presumably, indicate something, even if only that for political commentators the figure of 1·6 million unemployed represented the threshold of perception of questions which had not been seriously put since the inter-war years: about the social and political tolerances involved when unemployment rises far beyond recent historical experience, and about the value of bland hopes (expressed as recently as the early July NEDC meeting not only by Treasury Ministers and CBI but also TUC representatives) that after the coming hard times, employment would naturally be restored to its former levels.

The last occasion on which Cabinet Ministers discussed the problem of mass unemployment, on a rising curve, backed by a world slump, was in the lifetime of the Labour administration, 1929–31; if the two other 1980 phenomena of induced deflation and technological change are included, then the date should be pushed back to September 1921 when unemployment stood at 12·9 per cent. of the insured labour force and Lloyd George planned an extensive scheme of relief with the co-operation of businessmen, bankers and trade union officials, supported by substantial state funds. However, before asking what comparisons can be made with the last period of habitual high unemployment, it is worth looking at present totals and at disaggregated figures rather than global ones because of variables such as school leavers, those near retirement, the short-term

* The author is Reader in Modern History, University of Sussex; and his last two books are *Politics in Industrial Society* and *Power and the Party: Changing Faces of Communism in Western Europe*: both Andre Deutsch, 1980.

out of work, and the inclusion or not of Northern Ireland, which help to cause economists' models to give such a wide range of forecasts. Global projections do, however, all indicate that the rate of increase in long-term unemployment is rapid (those under 60 years old unemployed for at least four months, 1,180,000 in June compared with 306,000 in December 1973—for at least six months 600,000 compared with 200,000); and that Britain should be compared with Italy and perhaps France, not Germany, Belgium or Holland.

Regional Differences

The geography of unemployment follows quite closely the classic pattern of the interwar years: South-West Scotland, North and South Wales, the North East and the Liverpool area have now been joined by Cornwall; as yet both East and West Midlands have borne up surprisingly well. A recent Department of Employment prediction on the basis of 2 million and 2·5 million unemployed, however, gave in the case of 2 million, over 10 per cent. out of work for all North England, Scotland, Wales; near 10 per cent. West Midlands, Yorkshire, Humberside; 5–6 per cent. the South and East; in the 2·5 million case, over 11 per cent. for all these areas, except the last, with peaks of 14–15 per cent. in North Wales, 16 per cent. Northern Ireland, and nearly 20 per cent. in regions such as Liverpool, Hartlepool and Lanarkshire. Looking at specific industries, the latest Manpower Survey of Employment Prospects, covering the experience of some 1,600 companies, also states that " more employers are planning cuts in the labour force than at any time in the last 14 years ". There is " the possibility of a dramatic increase in labour shedding throughout British industry ". The survey is also gloomy about the Midlands, particularly light and electrical engineering and chemical manufacturing. But what stands out most clearly from their figures and the Department's breakdown by industry is the degree to which private companies have suffered more in each region than the public sector. Whereas construction unemployment, always a good indicator of the length and depth of a recession, is already high, very high in the hardest hit regions, in certain public cases such as gas, water and electricity, unemployment is as low as 2 per cent. That local authorities generally have also resisted redundancies suggests how government intentions have been evaded, Manchester being an apposite example. In complete contrast, as the Manpower report points out, " employers (in the private sector) may now be more experienced in facing recession and in taking decisive action "—that is, by shedding labour.

These phenomena of high regional differences, the exposure of old manufacturing industry and relative security of the public service, had their counterparts in the interwar years. On the other hand, the burden then did not fall especially heavily on the under 25s as it does now, nor on ethnic minorities, particularly Blacks (among whom unemployment in June 1980 was 26 per cent. higher than in 1979). Heavy long-term structural unemployment, concentrated on the staple industries, heavy engineering, iron and steel, textiles, coal-mining and ship-building, hit the mature and elderly almost indiscriminantly and conditions actually encouraged the employment of apprentices—at least, that is, until they qualified for a man's wage, when employers tended immediately to put them out of work.

With the possible exception of the Black communities and parts of inner cities such as Liverpool, the levels of despair and misery in the 1930s cannot be compared with 1980 as even a cursory reading of the literature shows. George Orwell or Wal Hannington, Walter Greenwood or Lewis Grassic Gibbon described a world which literally cannot be revived, in which the out of work were kept immobile by lack of education or alternative opportunity, stultified in the apathy of whole cities, and fenced off from effective protest by a dole system carefully tuned to minimum needs. There was, of course, another face of the 1930s: the relative prosperity of the South East and the Midlands, of new consumer-directed, capital-intensive industries, or old ones which had undergone rationalisation and renovation in the late 1920s, which was psychologically as well as geographically remote from the Distressed Areas. Hence the Hunger Marches with their pathetic aim of telling the rest of England what life beyond the pale of employment meant. This old division, a separation of much of England from the rest of Britain is, however, already recurring, and with it some of the political chimeras characteristic of the 1930s—about the young losing the will to work or the long-term unemployed falling prone to extremist political programmes. But in making very general comparisons it should be remembered that the number of insured workers is today much higher so that a figure of 15 per cent. out of work in 1980 compares with 10 per cent. in 1930, but also that the 1930s were not years of inflation. Wages and prices remained remarkably stable from 1927 to 1940, whatever the unemployment figures, with wages drawing just ahead after 1930 (a factor which helps to explain why those on the right side of the job line found the decade relatively prosperous). For a fairer comparison with 1980 one should go back to 1921, the point at which rapid wage and price inflation turned into slump, and unemployment was first seriously affected by technological change and government-inspired deflation.

Technological Change

Technological change brought about not only redistribution between industries—growth of the light engineering, electrical, motor car, consumer goods or chemicals industries and the whole tertiary and distribution sector, at the expense of the staples, such as coal mining where employment fell from $1\frac{1}{4}$ million in 1918 to 950,000 in 1930—but between levels of industry. Thus the white-collar sector (ranging from managers down to shop assistants) grew from 21·2 per cent. of the total in 1921 to 23 per cent. 10 years later, at a time when manual workers fell from 72 per cent. to 70 per cent., the decline of job opportunities being most acute among skilled men. Meanwhile deflation manifested itself in various ways such as the assault on State spending, particularly on education; health pro-vision and housing, associated with the 1921 Committee on National Expenditure (the notorious " Geddes Axe "); Treasury budgetary policy and the drive to return to the Gold Standard at the pre-1914 parity; and the reluctance of government to engage either on public works for the relief of unemployment or to raise loans for aid to industry. All of this was detrimental to employment and (as Keynes pointed out when relating the new parity achieved in 1925 to the state of the coal industry) was sometimes directly responsible for throwing men out of work.

Today's anti-monetarists could make considerable play with the contrast between the oracular pronouncements of Treasury and Bank of England about the absolute need for deflation in the early and mid-1920s and the rough and ready way in which deflation actually took place at the hands of Churchill, a Chancellor who confessed his incompetence fully to understand the Gold Standard argument, and Montagu Norman, Governor of the Bank, whose direction has been compared (by Professor Donald Winch) to the " semi-instinctive skills of the craftsman ". At the very end of the decade the contrast was still exemplified by Sir Richard Hopkins' sophisticated evidence to the Macmillan Committee on why money for public works would be a diversion from " the normal supply of capital "; and by the crude fallacies of the 1930 May Committee on Expenditure. Never-theless, in terms of reducing wages, and to a slightly lesser extent, costs, and in raising the value of the pound against the dollar, the policy appeared to work. From 1922 wages remained stable, virtually down to the Second World War, and the cost of living fell slowly, at least until 1936. The price was unemployment, industrial strife and a high level of class conflict.

It is difficult to assess precisely how much unemployment was caused by deflation, rather than by technological change; furthermore, the onset of world depression in 1929–31 took the 1920's hard core of one million to over three million for a time. But economic historians agree that a different government policy in the 1920s would not only have mitigated the overall problem, but ameliorated the specific effects of technological change, and achieved higher overall growth rates. It is only necessary to point to the experience of Britain's competitors in the 1920s, or to what *was* done in the period of " rationalisation " after 1927 when wage-cutting, as a coherent policy shared alike by employers and Treasury, was largely set aside and when for a brief time before the depression, considerable progress was made in stagnant industries, by way of assisted finance for investment, mergers and the application of new techniques, backed by government's fiscal incentives.

The Path That Led to 1926

Political prejudice, of course, conditioned much of what was done in the name of sound economic doctrine. Two beliefs had become deeply entrenched among the members of Lloyd George's coalition as a result of the First World War and their experience of the need, after 1915, continually to bargain with the labour movement to gain the munitions supply and manpower needed for victory: first, that whatever the pre-war constitution appeared to indicate about the inviolability of parliamentary politics, " responsible labour " had to be bribed or bludgeoned into collaboration with the State in order to make the system work; and, conversely, that the autonomous power of " extremist, politically-inclined, organisations " such as the Triple Alliance (miners, railwaymen and transport workers) or the well-established Shop Stewards' Movement, was unconstitutional, dangerous, and had to be broken. The slow, erratic process of institutionalisation on both sides of industry, often government-aided, which led to the setting up of formal, centralised employers' organisations and the TUC General Council, and a form of co-operation in the late 1920s (which I have elsewhere called the beginnings of " corporate bias "), satisfied the first requirement. The second was met by the break-up of the Triple Alliance on Black Friday, in April 1921, and the disintegration of a Shop Stewards' Movement faced with mass unemployment.

139

But despite the necessity of collaboration with the TUC, strong anti-trade union feelings survived, accompanied by a lurid awareness of political threats from the Communist-backed Minority Movement, and the National Unemployed Workers' Movement (NUWM). Moreover, collaboration was not allowed to influence economic doctrine; the concerted policy of wage-cutting, which the Triple Alliance had tried to fight at the war's end by extending to national-isation State control of mines and railways, led eventually to the General Strike in 1926. That was, essentially, a defensive action in which the trades union movement fought on behalf of the miners chiefly because each union saw itself next in the line of attack.

Unemployment in the 1920s was thus inextricably linked with government deflation, industrial change, and conflict about power and cash relationships in industry. It is this combination which seems most in need of emphasis today, especially since the *later* 1920s brought about a reversal, with a Conservative Prime Minister and Minister of Labour (Baldwin and Steel-Maitland) bent on re-creating a working relationship with the TUC, despite the continu-ing anti-union bias of many other Ministers, and the ultramontane views of party delegates who demanded, and got, retribution for the General Strike in the form of the 1927 Trade Disputes Act. The TUC appeared to have lost the General Strike. Indeed, its member-ship declined from seven million in 1920 to four million in 1930. Yet, as government suspected and the leaders of employers con-federations discovered, industrial regeneration in the late 1920s could not be carried through without union collaboration, granted only on the tacit assumption that wage-cutting would be abandoned. Even the unemployed found a champion in Lloyd George with his Liberal inquiries into the state of the nation and the brilliant proto-Keynesian " We Can Conquer Unemployment " which, in the 1929 election, put both Tory Government and Labour Opposition on the defensive.

This turn-about did not occur by accident. Again, it was possible for advocates of deflation to conclude that monetary policy had done the job: industrial militancy did decline: 1919 had seen 34 million days lost in strikes, 1921 85 million. If 1926 is ignored as excep-tional, each succeeding year brought a fall, down to a mere one million in 1927. But this was to ignore the complexity of causes and effects. The political threat presented by the million unemployed either in terms of unquiet public opinion, demonstrated during the 1929 election campaign, or Communist organisation of the unem-ployed, may have been a lesser cause than wider changes in the views of employers, Ministers, civil servants and trade unionists themselves. But the absence of *effective* protest was due partly to the labour movement itself. One result of the growth of a TUC General Council, bent on negotiating with government and employers, had been the marginalisation by unions themselves of shop stewards' activity and anything remotely to do with the Communist Party. So the Conservative or Labour Governments could count on the TUC to fight this particular battle for them. Whatever form it took, as Minority Movement, NUWM, Hunger Marches, Councils of Action, the Communist Party's industrial organisation was exposed by the TUC as deviation from the proper course of political action based on parliamentary politics and led by the Labour Party—even when, to the grave embarrassment of the General Council, the CPGB advocated " all power to the General Council " before the General Strike.

Lack of a Mass Movement

From 1928 Comintern instructions ensured that the CPGB and its offshoots among the unemployed struggled alone. Meanwhile TUC efforts to build up a " legitimate " presence among the out of work continued. On Trades Councils, now largely subordinated to General Council instructions, TUC-inspired organisations were set up to combat the NUWM and to recruit new union members from among the non-unionised unemployed. When the CPGB changed its mind in 1934 and again called for United Front tactics, the TUC renewed its anti-extremist fervour with publication of the so-called " Black Circular ", outlawing Communist or Fascist members from any union post, or Trades Council office.

Even without TUC hostility, it would have been hard, in the interwar years, to organise the unemployed for political protest. None of the Hunger Marches before 1934 was attended on the way south by more than a few hundred. The loss of workplace or union as a focus for activity, the onset of apathy, disorientation, undernourishment, combined with a low level of political education, geographical fragmentation and incompatibility between stratified groups of unemployed workers, all militated against the creation of a mass movement *from below*. To these should be added the failure of political parties other than the CPGB or Independent Labour Party (which disaffiliated from the Labour Party in 1932) to offer much alternative, and the peculiarly sharp distinction between those in work and those out; between North and South; and between the declining industries on one hand, the profitable sectors and the service industries, whether public or private on the other. The securely employed did well on balance and had few grievances between 1926 and 1939. The unemployed found themselves isolated, failed not only by their former unions, but by the main political parties and the employed majority of a supposedly politically coherent working class.

Today's Organisation of the Unemployed

Today, the TUC shows itself much more concerned. The Labour Party, rent as it is by faction, finds a precarious unity in the House of Commons on this one issue. The far Left is hopelessly divided. The Communist Party is split between Euro-communists and Stalinists. The grupuscules, SWP or WSL fight their sectarian battles. Government deflation (for that is what, in this context, monetarist policy amounts to) launched on top of the growing trend of techno-logical unemployment, combined with the effects of a world depres-sion and an over-valued currency, will ensure rapidly rising unem-ployment for at least another 18 months. Inflationary wage settle-ments seem likely to persist where the more powerful trade unions are concerned, and a continuing high level of industrial conflict may encourage a greater measure of militancy among those who would otherwise have had their aspirations depressed. But does all that presage an organisation of the unemployed more successful than in the 1920s and 1930s, a force which could combine with public anxiety, and action by Labour Party and TUC to deflect the govern-ment's economic strategy? And even if it does not, what might the longer-term consequences of such mass unemployment be, in the light of historical experience?

In *The Lion and the Unicorn*, George Orwell pointed to defer-ence, respect for the law and established order, and sharp social stratification as dominant characteristics of the British working class. That these still exist is demonstrated by much recent socio-logical research and by the absence or low level of industrial violence (compared, say, with France) at times of considerable stress such as the winters of 1973–74 or 1978–79. The amazement of flying pickets at the behaviour of Sheerness workers, and their apparent ignorance of the political culture of working-class solidarity during the last steel strike, suggests that geographical fragmentation remains strong, just as the experience of disorientation is reaffirmed by studies among skilled newly unemployed of South Shields or East Kilbride.

So far, it appears, countervailing action by the State has been effective, not only through YOP, STEP or MSC (and it is worth remembering that, even during the deflation of 1976–78, the Chancellor, Denis Healey, always insisted on and got as much funding as MSC required, with the result that the Labour government was seen to be doing something to check the ravages of its policy on the unemployed) but Government propaganda. In Ministers' speeches, whatever their variations on the theme of sympathy, unemployment always appears as the necessary consequence of an incontestable and therefore virtuous economic law. On the other hand, unemployment now threatens expectations which are much higher and have been sustained over a far longer time—since the 1940s—than in any previous period of industrial history. One very recent inquiry [1] shows that benefit for the average unemployed male averages 44 per cent. of previous earnings; and that although the low-paid tend to be put out of work first, it is the higher paid for whom the difference is greatest. Apart from steel workers, few of the redundant collect large cash payments. Over half of those studied were finding it hard to cope, and falling behind already with bills, rent, mortgage. Relative deprivation affects individuals better-educated and probably more politically aware than in the interwar years, less culturally deferential, more prone to what radicals tend to call " a state of desubordination ",[2] wide open to factious appeals from extremists of left or right.

The attractions of radicalism or nihilism may be greater at a time when the impact has fallen with peculiar severity on the young. Even before the July rush of school leavers, nearly 250,000 under 19 were out of work, according to MSC figures—three times the 1974 total. Of those under 25, in June 13½ per cent. were unemployed, in contrast to 4½ per cent. of the 25–54 age group. If the global figure rises to 2 million, then the under-25s will be 17 per cent. (700,000); if 2·5 million, over 20 per cent. (900,000). In Europe these figures could be compared only to Italy. The difference between young and mature will, of course, be aggravated if YOP and MSC support tapers off, as it is bound to do, despite Mr. Prior's pledge to add some 50,000 places by next year. For MSC's staff and budget have been severely cut back; and YOP's efficiency at placing the young in permanent jobs must inevitably decline during recession,

[1] By David J. Smith, of the Policy Studies Institute, in *Policy Studies* (September 1980).
[2] Ralph Miliband's phrase. It is worth recalling that, commentating on the use of the armed forces in strikes, in the year 1919, the CIGS remarked that it had worked well before the 1914 war " but at that time we had a well-disciplined and ignorant army, whereas now we have an army educated and ill-disciplined ".

given that the job market is increasingly prejudiced against them because of what employers, with considerable justification, regard as their excessively high initial wages and their levels of skill lower than those of mature competitors.

During the 1920s the indifference of public opinion, and in particular of the Press as an expression of that opinion, accentuated the isolation of the unemployed except in cases such as the distress of Welsh miners during the 1926 strike, which occasioned the Lord Mayor's Fund. Not until about 1934 did a mood of sympathetic concern develop—more or less at the moment when the slump began to lift from London and the South-East—so that the 1934 Hunger March was given a quite different reception from any of its predecessors. Today, the newspapers proclaim the connection between deflation and unemployment and industrial decay, and speculate on the likelihood of social upheaval. The public may still be persuaded by neo-classical economic arguments, but the latest Gallup Poll (July 15) showed that the numbers worried by unemployment had doubled since May, to 49 per cent.—at which level they surpassed those whose chief concern was inflation.

But self-interest may also operate in a different way from the late 1920s when wage rates ran almost level with the cost of living. Today's wage-earners still take their assumptions from a recent golden age, 1950–65. They probably voted for the Conservatives in order to regain conditions lost in the inflationary 1970s, and they will not be pleased if their standard of life has not risen by the next election. Most will not vote Conservative again if real wages have actually been lowered, as is the clear intention of government policy at present. Whatever the constraints imposed by fear of unemployment in the short run, it is highly unrealistic to assume any long-term change in patterns of wage-bargaining behaviour which have taken nearly 40 years to develop; or to hope that, whatever had happened earlier, rising money wage rates could be contained in the run-up to a 1984 election.

The Immediate Future

It seems possible, therefore, that unemployment will continue to be both a source of fear yet an inadequate deterrent once the immediate recession is past, and that this can only be a recipe for political unrest. In addition, the present cycle has been superimposed on a much broader change in underlying assumptions, which again resembles the early 1920s. The three cardinal tenets of post-war political consensus have been largely if not wholly abandoned during the last seven years. Full employment as a governing principle in political economy slipped in the early 1970s but was only downgraded finally after 1974 when Labour Government policy, giving priority to recovering price and wage stability, and the maintenance of living standards for those in work, paralleled the trend towards declining employment in manufacturing industry and growth in the service and public sector.

Secondly, the level of ideological conflict, whose absence had characterised the whole post-war period, rose steadily to engulf both major political parties and accentuate differences within the trade union movement and employers' organisations. Increasingly, views about conflict, and the struggle between capital and labour, which had once seemed archaic if not actually moribund, have been revived and legitimised. As an almost inevitable third factor, the present Government has, consciously and deliberately, withdrawn from its long-held part as begetter of the triangular system of industrial politics, leaving NEDC a mere shell, with CBI and TUC leaders floundering.

The confusion and complexity of responses to mass unemployment, however, prevent any simple conclusion that political and ideological conflict in the manner of the early 1920s is inevitable. In government, the orthodoxy associated with Treasury Ministers, and of course the Prime Minister—that things are getting better, that inflation, wage demands, and trade union militancy are declining, and that there is no possibility of change in an incontrovertibly correct policy—is contested not only by Keynesians and Tory Radicals, but by Minister's own actions: the baling out of Harland and Wolff or the reprieves for steel factories, and the defence orders placed, at higher cost, in Britain rather than the United States.

There are also two lines of argument among the Conservative " opposition " which have not been specifically repudiated: the point made by Peter Walker in a speech to the Tory Reform Group that the sheer cost of unemployment benefit will add such billions to public borrowing that the Chancellor may have to relinquish the PSBR target for 1981–82; and Sir Ian Gilmour's mordant remark: " it would be foolish to think we can forget the political consequences of what we do ". But there are no fundamental alternatives: whatever Mr. Prior does to broaden the YOP programme, or find more money for MSC, the Department of Employment has not as yet set itself up against the Treasury over major budget priorities.

Nor is there much sign of the sort of conjuncture between dissident Ministers and party officials as occurred in 1922, when the Lloyd George coalition collapsed; although in July a survey of Conservative Area Chairmen showed substantial disquiet in all regions except the South-East. Very few Conservative M.P.s are prepared to dissent from the view that " trade union power " has to be tamed in order to create the conditions for a private, manufacturing industry-led boom: which are lower real wages, a pool of skilled unemployed, and trades union willingness to accept changes in work organisation and production.

This is the reality behind the disputes over clause 17 of the Employment Bill—which is itself secondary to the main argument about distribution of power in industry. Only after some evidence has been given of unions becoming more flexible, less immunised from the " real " world, could change occur; even then, in default of a wages policy, unemployment is likely to remain the chief deterrent, whether or not the TUC General Council is readmitted to a share in policy-making and institutional collaboration.

A very large revision of recent history is involved here, far more damaging than anything Harold Wilson said about the " 13 wasted years " and rarely made explicit. It is held to justify the ending, indeed repudiation, of post-war consensus. From the period 1945–75 it is deduced: (1) that in a tight labour market, with trades union monopoly power and employers' willingness to pay inflationary wages (particularly in the motor-car industry, where the annual round originated) Beveridge's nightmare of wage inflation allied to declining profits came true; (2) that government's incapacity was exposed, because of political fears about conflict: even the Macmillan era witnessed a surrender to trade union power, notably in 1957 when the engineering employers were prevented by Cabinet from fighting a long strike; (3) that Treasury Ministers (with the exception of Thorneycroft, who was sacked in the crucial confrontation of 1957) failed, wilfully, to control money supply, under the illusion that expanding it would allow growth to continue at higher prices.

The Civil Service's Involvement

Departmental views about unemployment suggest not only a reluctance to envisage its political repercussions, based on the assumption that it is no longer so great a bogey as in the past, and that having passed 1·5 million there is now no normative limit of tolerance, but also the disappearance of traditional functional differences between ministries. (For half a century, from 1920, Treasury views tended on such issues to coincide with those of the financial community, Board of Trade/Industry with business, and Labour with the TUC). As far as one can see, the only distinction now is that the Employment team would like to do more for job creation, but will not, in any circumstances, ask for anything which would involve spending money and incurring Treasury disapproval.

This is perhaps not so much a symptom of pusillanimity as of recoil in Whitehall, after years of criticism by both parties and individual Ministers, of civil servants' role in policy-making and their alleged emasculation of party manifestos; criticism which has culminated in the Tory assault on an overblown bureaucracy, and the Labour Left's polemic against a State threat to civil liberty. Seeing themselves set up as scapegoats, and unquestionably fearing Number 10, many civil servants not unnaturally wish to lie low, with the consequence that they are unlikely to take initiatives to forestall trouble. Let Ministers who create a mess clear it up; the apparatus will do merely what it is told, and present itself to whatever Government takes over next, without prejudice. It is in this sense that recent Treasury papers apparently display forecasts based on as yet unproved assumptions about change in, for example, wage bargaining patterns, relegating to footnotes the figures civil servants actually believe in, derived from more traditional models.

Meanwhile, CBI and TUC each display a duality as old as their institutional history, members of each reverting to old-fashioned, explicitly ideological judgments about the " Opposition ", and the " natural antipathy " between capital and labour. Both have been criticised from below for corporatist behaviour—the CBI at its first National Conference over the pay bargaining scheme, and the TUC for its attempts to hang on to vestigial contact with the Government. The majority of leaders of both nevertheless remain committed to an overall doctrine of industrial interdependence, to which ideological conflict and unemployment represent appalling threats. But leaders of the trade unions are probably under much greater pressure from below, and some members of the CBI Council are deeply worried that their power within their own unions may be permanently weakened, as much by the attitudes displayed towards the TUC by government in discussion, as by the radical left, or semi-autonomous shop stewards' groups, or just the mass of trades union members, angry at falling living standards, or frightened by the spread of industrial decay. The " day of action " in June, in private admitted as retrograde, was presented to the rank and file as evidence of " struggle ", without making a complete rupture with government. But by the winter of 1980–81 it may be too late, even on NEDC, to recover the TUC's commitment to interdependence without which, in the opinion of very many employers, the necessary changes in industrial patterns of behaviour cannot be achieved.

TUC and the Unemployed

There is thus a substantial chance that the present inextricably linked phenomena of deflation, unemployment, recession, technological change and political polarisation will further disrupt the post-war political consensus, and create the conditions for unprecedented social unrest. (Recent French history, since introduction of the Plan Barre, and events in Italy since 1976, give this prediction weight.) If so, then 1920s evidence suggests that it would take shape partly at regional level, through the growth of spontaneous movements around workplace or union centres (and in this case without Communist affiliation as a ban to wider sympathy) and partly through intervention from above, by Labour Party and TUC, intended to control and prevent them getting out of hand as the Councils of Action did in 1921.

Something like the former has already occurred in Newcastle, where an " unemployed union ", with an informal structure run by former shop stewards and union officials, has centred on the local authority's employment office and worked with NALGO opposing cuts in the health service. Although only in embryo, such an organisation presents fewer obstacles to a future Labour Party/TUC association; indeed the will to associate already exists: it aspires to affiliate to the local Trades Council and to an actual trades union. Whether the enormous leap of imagination that is required for the TUC actually to organise the unemployed, can be made is another question. It is one that has already been raised in Italy (by the Communist-dominated CGIL, which has nevertheless led it into conflict with the Italian Communist Party) and Belgium, without definitive solution. But Len Murray has already taken an initiative at the level of local union committees, to encourage trades unions to retain unemployed members at reduced subscriptions, and to keep in touch with them by passing on information about benefits and training schemes. It seems a more likely outcome than capture by one of the sectarian grupuscules, who would surely need the prior development of an autonomous shop stewards' movement—something which only occurred during the First World War. Their appeal may, however, be much greater to the young who have never been in employment or been inducted into a trades union, who in Italy in very large numbers have turned to the nihilists and the urban guerrillas.

If mass unemployment led to physical disorder there can be little doubt that the State would succeed in controlling or dissipating the opposition, as it did in the early 1920s. Unrest might indeed be welcomed on the right of the Conservative Party as justification for current preparations by the Civil Contingencies organisation, and as a tangible means of purging discontent, like lancing a boil, the better to heal it afterwards. But it is more likely that government will be faced sometime after 1980 with some form of organisation of the unemployed by TUC and Labour Party which is not violent but which is directed towards forms of political protest. This will restore much of the Party's lost unity and the TUC's political leverage and will emphasise not only the residual strength of the labour movement but its apparently organic and total opposition to this Government and its economic policy.

By then it may be too late to think of reviving NEDC as a forum for genuine collaboration. It is also conceivable that TUC and CBI might, on certain issues, have ganged up together: and not only against high interest rates and subsidised imports. Implicitly, already, the fact that many firms continue to meet wage claims around 20 per cent. indicates that employers and employed have a common interest greater, in employers' opinion, than the benefits to be obtained from wage-cutting by conflict. (More positive evidence about interdependence can be found in the Industrial Society's nine-point plan for more open communications and participation in management, signed, *inter alia*, by Sir Raymond Pennock, and Messrs. Chapple and Basnett.)

There are remedies, many of them less radical than the sudden reverses of policy demanded chiefly by Socialist economists (and for that reason, at least at present, inconceivable). In the short term and, one must presume, most acceptable in cash as well as political terms, come palliatives simply designed to ease the problem of unemployment for those groups most likely to cause trouble: primarily the young, through extensions of YOP, but also the mature unemployed through STEP and MSC, whose extra funding the Treasury might be prepared to accept, if only for the same reasons as it did when Mr. Healey was Chancellor.

Beyond that, it may become practical to talk of extending job release schemes (probably the most cost-effective measure), or early retirement which, despite its high cost in social security payments, offers the largest gain and the only one of real benefit in relation to the coming technological unemployment. It may even become possible to air schemes such as taking a percentage of wages in some or all industries to help state or co-operative investment in the regions, as is currently proposed for the Italian Mezzogiorno. And by then government may have accepted that TUC and CBI both have a vested interest in rationalising the pattern of employment as a whole, not only hours and conditions, but retirement and apprenticeship, participation in decision-making, location and production technology, for which NEDC appears the most suitable forum for discussion, just as the FBI/NCEO/TUC tripartite committee was in 1929–31.

But there are other political ramifications which ought not to be forgotten, during a process which at best would take three to five years. From the Government's point of view, the next election may, like that of 1929, be fought on the unemployment issue and commitment to the welfare state. Memory of the inter-war years' unemployment dogged the Conservative Party for a decade after 1940, as the Principal Agent's constituency review showed, shortly before the disastrous 1945 election. On present performance it seems likely that the repudiation of what was embodied in 30 years of Conservative history since the 1948 Industrial Charter cannot easily be remedied by Tory Radicals or Keynesians and must therefore, if at all, be offset by material gains—for which the probability is already becoming attenuated.

After all, will employment revive? As recently as March this year, *The Times* declared confidently: " as inflation slows, output and employment begin recovering and [the rise in unemployment] is followed by a much steeper reduction in unemployment later ". Such assertions, like that of the " change " in workers' behaviour, remain unproved. (Strikes, regular wage demands related to the cost of living, and insistence on wage differentials all resurfaced after nearly 20 years of high inter-war unemployment, and despite wartime emergency restrictions, introduced in 1940–41. Thoroughly to change attitudes and practices, especially in the sheltered public sector, unemployment may have to be prolonged for many years.) There are too many variables, some to do with the underlying extent of technological change, some with employers' own learning graph and determination to shed labour permanently, as they did in the rationalisation years 1927–30, in preference to mere wage-cutting.

The whole service and white-collar sector will look utterly different in less than 10 years as a result of the coming micro-chip office revolution. Given the nature of contemporary trades union organisation and practice, the worst of this will fall on the young, now aged 10 to 15.

Meanwhile, things which we have taken for granted may change. As Paul Addison has pointed out, one feature of the Second World War was that the State came to be seen by the vast majority of people as benevolent: the State, rather than the political parties, provided the welfare cushion against misfortune and the security of public sector employment. For those forced out of work today it may not matter greatly whether their sacrifice is made in the cause of economic orthodoxy, or as a result of technological change, or world recession. Their anger will focus on tangible things, and may conflate the responsibility. If the State came to be seen as unfeeling, even hostile, then " desubordination " and some of its by-products, such as the black economy would, indeed, be enhanced.

Finally, a question: what will Britain look like after even three years of 2 million unemployed? Divisions which for half a century governments have tried to abolish will show nakedly, between the two geographical Englands, with Scotland, Wales and Northern Ireland on the periphery, like the Italian Mezzogiorno; between those in work and the unemployed; between the mature and the young, between white and black. They already exist. If they are heightened by the sort of political conflict allied to a capital/labour antithesis which nearly every Conservative leader since Baldwin has tried to prevent, or by an unthinking and indiscriminate assault on trade unionism which confuses structural backwardness with moral turpitude, or by an intolerant repudiation of the post-war consensus rather than a reasoned attempt to find out what went wrong, then it will recall the old tag: " *Ubi solitudinem faciunt, pacem appellant* " —where they make a desert, they call it peace.